Where are the jobless?

Changing unemployment and non-employment in cities and regions

Anne E. Green and David Owen

First published in Great Britain in 1998 by

The Policy Press
University of Bristol
Rodney Lodge
Grange Road
Bristol BS8 4EA
UK
Tel no   +44 (0)117 973 8797
Fax no   +44 (0)117 973 7308
E-mail   tpp@bristol.ac.uk
http://www.bristol.ac.uk/Publications/TPP

In association with the Joseph Rowntree Foundation

ISBN 1 86134 100 8

Anne E. Green is Principal Research Fellow at the Institute for Employment Research, University of Warwick and **David Owen** is Senior Research Fellow at the Centre for Research in Ethnic Relations, University of Warwick.

The **Joseph Rowntree Foundation** has supported this project as part of its programme of research and innovative development projects, which it hopes will be of value to policy makers and practitioners. The facts presented and the views expressed in this report, however, are those of the authors and not necessarily those of the Foundation.

Cover design by Qube Design Associates, Bristol.
Printed in Great Britain by Hobbs the Printers, Southampton.

Contents

List of tables and figures iv
Acknowledgements vi
Executive summary vii

1 Introduction 1
Background 1
Structure of the report 1

2 The significance of unemployment and non-employment 3
Unemployment as a key policy issue 3
'New landscapes' of employment: implications for unemployment and non-employment 3
The geography of employment change 5

3 Measuring unemployment and non-employment 7
Conceptual issues in measuring unemployment and non-employment 7
Practical issues in measuring unemployment and non-employment 10
Geographical issues 11

4 Inter- and intra-urban variations in unemployment and non-employment 12
Introduction 12
Overview at national and regional scales 12
Local level variations 20

5 Dynamics of unemployment 33
Introduction 33
The likelihood of becoming and ceasing to be unemployed and unemployment duration 33
Longitudinal perspectives on unemployment 43

6 Match and mismatch 46
Introduction 46
Changing job profiles at the local level 47
Occupational profiles of the unemployed 53

7 Conclusions and policy implications 57
Introduction 57
A 'new' labour market – a 'new' broader approach 57
Broadening perspectives on joblessness – from unemployment to non-employment 58
The changing map of joblessness 59
Challenging spatial concentrations of joblessness 60
Research needs 62

References 63

Appendix A: Geographical frameworks 67
Appendix B: Producing local area estimates 69

List of tables and figures

Tables

1   Exemplar alternative indicators of unemployment and non-employment   9

2   Comparison of the main sources of unemployment data   10

3   Proportion of men not working in three large urban areas (%)   20

4   Unemployment and non-employment rates for persons of working age for TTWAs with largest increases in non-employment (1981-91) (%)   21

5   Unemployment and non-employment rates for men of working age for TTWAs with largest increases in non-employment (1981-91) (%)   23

6   Unemployment and non-employment rates for persons of working age for LADs with largest increases in non-employment (1981-91) (%)   23

7   Unemployment and non-employment rates for men of working age for LADs with largest increases in non-employment (1981-91) (%)   24

8   Likelihood of becoming and ceasing to be unemployed in three large urban areas and Great Britain (%)   35

9   Distribution of TTWAs by quadrant on the basis of the likelihood of becoming and ceasing to be unemployed (Winter 1992/93 and Winter 1995/96)   35

10 TTWAs ranked on male long-term unemployment rate (April 1991 and April 1997) (%)   37

11 Median duration of completed unemployment spells by LAD 'families' (weeks)   42

12 Change in employment by TTWA (1981-91)   47

13 Change in employment by LAD 'family' (1981-91)   48

14 Change in structure of employment by LAD 'family' (1981-91)   48

15 Projected decline and growth in employment by industry (1994-2005)   50

16 Projected decline and growth in employment by occupation (1994-2005)   51

17 Comparison of employment trends in other (unskilled) occupations and professional occupations (1981-2005)   52

18 Comparison of employment trends for men and women (1981-2005)   52

Figures

1   Conventional categorisation of employment, unemployment and inactivity   8

2   ILO unemployment levels by gender, Great Britain (1984-96)   13

3   ILO unemployment rates by gender, Great Britain (1984-96)   13

4   Inactivity rates for men by age group, Great Britain (1984-96)   14

5   Inactivity rates for women by age group, Great Britain (1984-96)   14

6   Non-employment rates for working age population by gender, Great Britain (1984-96) — 15

7   Indices of ILO unemployment rates for men by region (1984-96) — 16

8   Indices of non-employment rates for men by region (1984-96) — 17

9   Indices of inactivity rates for men by region (1984-96) — 18

10 Unemployment and non-employment rates among older men in Merseyside (1977-95) — 22

11 Unemployment, inactivity and non-employment rates for men of working age by LAD 'families' (1981 and 1991) — 25

12 Levels of unemployment and inactivity among men of working age by LAD 'families' (1981 and 1991) — 25

13 Unemployment, inactivity and non-employment rates for women of working age by LAD 'families' (1981 and 1991) — 26

14 Levels of unemployment and inactivity among women of working age by LAD 'families' (1981 and 1991) — 27

15 Unemployment, inactivity and non-employment rates for men of working age by ward (1981 and 1991) — 28

16 Unemployment, inactivity and non-employment rates for men aged 45-59 years by ward (1981 and 1991) — 29

17 Unemployment, inactivity and non-employment rates for women of working age by ward (1981 and 1991) — 30

18 The incidence of male unemployment in Merseyside (1991) — 31

19 The incidence of male unemployment in the West Midlands Metropolitan County (1991) — 31

20 The incidence of male unemployment in London (1991) — 32

21 Interrelationships between the likelihood of becoming unemployed and ceasing to be unemployed — 34

22 Likelihood of becoming unemployed and ceasing to be unemployed by TTWA (Winter 1992/93) — 36

23 Likelihood of becoming unemployed and ceasing to be unemployed by TTWA (Winter 1995/96) — 36

24 The duration profile of unemployment, Great Britain (1979-97) — 38

25 The incidence of longer-term unemployment by TTWA class (1991) — 39

26 The incidence of longer-term unemployment by TTWA class (1997) — 39

27 The incidence of male long-term unemployment in Merseyside (1991) — 40

28 The incidence of male long-term unemployment in the West Midlands Metropolitan County (1991) — 41

29 The incidence of male long-term unemployment in London (1991) — 41

30 Frequency distribution of unemployment spells (1982-97) — 43

31 Mean number of unemployment spells by age and gender (1982-97) — 44

32 Occupational profile of the unemployed by SOC Major Group, Merseyside (October 1997) — 54

33 Occupational profile of the unemployed by SOC Major Group, Inner London (October 1997) — 55

Acknowledgements

This research made use of data from the Censuses of Population for 1981 and 1991. Census data are Crown Copyright, and are made available to the academic community via an Economic and Social Research Council (ESRC)/ Joint Information Systems Committee (JISC) purchase. Of the other data sources used, the annual and quarterly Labour Force Surveys and the Joint Unemployment and Vacancies Operating System (JUVOS) Cohort Study (all also Crown Copyright), were deposited with the Data Archive for use by the academic sector by the Office for National Statistics (ONS). Official unemployment and long-term unemployment data for labour market and small areas were obtained using NOMIS (National Online Manpower Information System).

In creating estimates of change in labour market variables from Census data between 1981 and 1991, use was made of two data sets created by Daniel Dorling and his colleagues, made available by them via the MIDAS (University of Manchester) computer service. The first was a set of 1991 Census data reaggregated to 1981 ward boundaries. The second was a 'look-up file' detailing the location of 1991 Census enumeration districts within 1981 Census wards.

The project also made use of the Local Economy Forecasting Model, jointly developed by the Institute for Employment Research at the University of Warwick and Cambridge Econometrics.

In undertaking this research for the Joseph Rowntree Foundation the researchers have drawn on expertise developed over the years on a number of other projects funded by a range of sponsors, including the Department for Education and Employment, the ESRC (in particular grant reference number R000236608), the Leverhume Trust, the Government Office for Merseyside and the Joseph Rowntree Foundation.

Executive summary

Introduction

Unemployment remains at the top of the policy agenda, and the unemployment rate is one of the most widely used economic and social indicators. A variety of labour market programmes and changes in social security systems have been introduced in attempts to reduce unemployment and tackle problems of labour market disadvantage and social exclusion.

The aim of this study is to chart the changing geography of unemployment and non-employment in Britain in the 1980s and 1990s by manipulating, integrating and analysing information from a range of secondary data sources at regional, inter- and intra-urban scales, in order to answer two key questions:

- *Where* are the unemployed and non-employed?

- Have the unemployed and non-employed become more concentrated, and if so, where?

A secondary objective is to review patterns of employment change, and to examine the extent of 'mismatch' between the characteristics of the unemployed and available jobs.

Labour market developments – 'new landscapes' of employment

The labour market is the arena where changes in the economic environment, social trends and demographic developments come together to create 'new landscapes' of employment (and non-employment). Key features of these 'new landscapes' include the demise of jobs in manufacturing, a greater premium on higher level skills and a reduction in employment opportunities for those with no or few formal qualifications, the growth in 'flexible' working, an increase in the number of women in employment and the entrenchment of high levels of unemployment and non-participation – particularly among some sub-groups of the population and in some areas.

Debates on the geography of employment change have highlighted both regional and urban–rural dimensions of change. Increasing policy attention has been focused on social and spatial polarisation within cities resulting from economic restructuring. Across Europe there is a wish to avoid the worst excesses of the 'Americanisation' of cities, characterised by spatial concentrations of long-term unemployment and joblessness.

Measuring unemployment and non-employment

Despite the continuing policy concern about the persistence of high levels of unemployment, and the widespread use of the unemployment rate as a socioeconomic indicator, the task of defining and measuring unemployment in a clear and non-ambiguous fashion is problematic.

Conventionally, the adult population is divided into three labour market categories:

- the *employed*: those who have a paid job in an employee or self-employed capacity, or who are on government-supported training and employment programmes;

- the *unemployed*: those who do not have a job but who are available to take up a job;

- the *inactive*: all remaining members of the adult population, some of whom may want a job and some of whom do not want a job.

In reality, rather than neatly bounded categories there is a continuum from 'complete employment' to 'complete non-employment', with 'unemployment' in between. In order to get a more complete picture of changes in *how many* people are excluded from employment *where*, it is necessary to extend the analysis beyond unemployment to non-employment.

The geography of change in unemployment and non-employment

At the *national* level unemployment in Great Britain rose steadily in the early 1980s, peaked at 3 million in the middle of the decade, fell to less than 2 million in 1990, and rose again to over 2.8 million in 1993, before declining steadily once again. Over the same period inactivity rates rose for men and fell for women.

Most areas in Britain shared in these broad trends, though to varying extents. London stands out as suffering a deterioration in its unemployment situation relative to the national average. At the *regional* level, there is some evidence for convergence in unemployment rates. But no clear converging trend is apparent for non-employment, because inactivity rates increased more in the traditionally 'high unemployment' than in the traditionally 'low unemployment' areas. The result is a growing gap between unemployment and non-employment rates for men.

At the *local* level unemployment, inactivity and non-employment rates for men of working age are highest in Inner London and mining and industrial areas. The incidence of non-employment is higher in urban centres than in rural areas. In Inner London an increase in the unemployment rate contributed to the increase in non-employment between 1981 and 1991, but in the mining and industrial areas the entire growth in non-employment is accounted for by the increase in inactivity.

At the *micro area* level geographical variations in the experience of unemployment, inactivity

and joblessness are even more pronounced, with largest increases in unemployment, and especially in inactivity and non-employment, in the neighbourhoods – particularly those in inner-city areas and in concentrations of public sector housing – where the initial incidence was highest.

Unemployment dynamics

The stock of unemployment is in a constant state of flux. The size of the stock is determined by flows into and out of unemployment and the average duration of unemployment spells.

Those urban areas with the most severe unemployment problems (such as Merseyside) are characterised by a higher than average likelihood of entering unemployment and a lower than average likelihood of leaving unemployment. Problems of long duration unemployment are most severe in the metropolitan areas of northern Britain – particularly in the inner urban areas.

Analysis of longitudinal data on unemployment spells shows that a lower than average proportion of those leaving unemployment in large urban areas enter work. Those previously in unskilled occupations are also characterised by longer than average unemployment durations, and a smaller than average share of off-flows from unemployment into work (as opposed to other destinations).

Skills and spatial mismatches

A structural perspective on the causes of urban unemployment/joblessness places emphasis on *mismatch* between available jobs and the potential workers available to do those jobs. It is useful to make a distinction between:

- *skills* mismatch: focusing on *who* the unemployed are and the (im)balance between their characteristics and the attributes required by available jobs;

- *spatial* mismatch: focusing on *where* the unemployed are and the geographical mismatch between their residences and potential workplaces.

Conclusions and policy issues

The main conclusion of this study is that in the context of labour market developments in the 1980s and 1990s it is important to extend the focus of policy beyond unemployment in order to tackle joblessness. In general, the greater the degree of labour market disadvantage in an area, the smaller the proportion of people who would like work who are included within conventional definitions of unemployment.

From a policy perspective there is increasing recognition that a 'new' approach is needed, encompassing a broader range of policies to address a wider set of interrelated problems. The buzzwords of the 'new' approach are 'skills', 'employability', 'adaptability' and 'flexibility'. There is an emphasis on spatial targeting and policy delivery within a multiagency partnership framework. Nevertheless, a number of key issues and questions remain, including:

- How can the disaffection and apathy that is rife in areas of persistent high unemployment and non-employment be tackled?

- Can/will there be sufficient local and individual customisation of 'Welfare to Work' policies, and will there be enough 'quality opportunities' available to cater for the long-term unemployed in areas of highest non-employment and demand deficiency?

- In such areas will there be sufficient support at the local level, over a sufficiently long period of time, to enable the development of structures necessary for participation in economic development, and the integration of economic development with employment policy?

From a research perspective there is a need for more effort to be given to:

- monitoring and analysis of the size and nature of flows between employment, unemployment and inactivity at local level;

- development of monitoring and evaluation frameworks and systems for measuring the outputs and outcomes of labour market programmes to combat unemployment and non-employment.

Introduction

Background

Unemployment remains at the top of the policy agenda. A wide variety of labour market programmes and changes in social security systems have been introduced in attempts to reduce unemployment and tackle problems of labour market disadvantage and exclusion. Although there is widespread concern about the persistence of high levels of unemployment, and the uneven distribution of unemployment between population sub-groups and areas, the task of defining and measuring unemployment in a clear and non-ambiguous fashion is a problematic one. In the face of these difficulties, a key feature of the analyses presented in this study is that the focus of attention moves beyond 'unemployment' to 'non-employment', thus providing a more complete picture of 'joblessness'.

The aim of the study is simple: to provide an overview of the changing geography of unemployment and non-employment in Britain, by manipulating, integrating and analysing information from a range of secondary data sources to provide estimates of unemployment and non-employment for a hierarchy of geographical levels. In so doing, it is hoped that the analyses presented will provide a 'backcloth' for more detailed case studies in specific local areas, as well as yielding important policy-relevant findings more generally. The main objective is to chart the spatial incidence of unemployment and non employment at regional, inter- and intra-urban levels in the 1980s and 1990s. Secondary objectives are to review patterns of employment change, and to examine the extent of 'mismatch' between the characteristics of the unemployed and available jobs.

Structure of the report

This report is structured around five main themes:

- the salience of unemployment and non-employment in policy terms in the face of changes in the quantity, quality and distribution of employment;

- the measurement of unemployment and non-employment;

- the changing geography of unemployment and non-employment;

- the dynamics of unemployment and non-employment;

- the (mis)match between jobs and the jobless.

The continuing significance of unemployment as a key policy issue in economic and social terms is outlined in Chapter 2, with reference to prevailing conditions and ongoing debates about the degree, extent and causes of joblessness in Britain, Europe and North America. The main features of employment change in western societies generally, and in Britain in particular, are reviewed, and the characteristics of 'winners' and 'losers' from these trends are identified. Particular attention is paid to growing concerns about the geographical dimensions of socioeconomic change, especially regarding the plight of 'urban areas in difficulty', in the face of an overriding policy emphasis on supply-side perspectives.

Despite the policy significance and widespread use of indicators of unemployment, the task of measuring unemployment in a clear and unambiguous fashion is notoriously difficult.

Indeed, changes in the nature of employment mean that measurement issues are becoming even more problematic. In Chapter 3 both conceptual and practical issues relating to the measurement of unemployment using available data sources are reviewed. The scope and coverage of some of the key secondary data sources used to measure unemployment and non-employment are outlined, with reference to the range of geographical frameworks and units used in the analyses.

The main substantive analyses of the changing geography of unemployment and non-employment are presented in Chapter 4. The purpose of this chapter is to present a sequence of 'snapshots' of unemployment and non-employment at various geographical scales – from the national and regional levels to the local and micro area levels, in order to answer two key questions:

- *Where* are the unemployed and non-employed?

- Have the unemployed and non-employed become more concentrated, and if so, *where?*

While the emphasis in Chapter 4 is on 'stocks', in Chapter 5 some analyses of 'flow' and unemployment 'duration' statistics are presented in order to provide some insights into the dynamics of unemployment and non-employment. The main emphasis here is on the likelihood of becoming and ceasing to be unemployed and on the 'destinations' of those leaving the unemployment count.

One of the common themes running through the literature on changes in employment, unemployment and non-employment is the *mismatch* between the characteristics of available jobs and of those individuals without jobs. Occupational, spatial and other dimensions of 'mismatch' are explored in Chapter 6, using data on the occupational profiles of the unemployed, and actual and projected changes in the quantity and structure of employment at the local level.

In conclusion, the need to move beyond unemployment to consider broader perspectives on joblessness is reiterated in Chapter 7, alongside other key policy issues emerging from the analyses.

The significance of unemployment and non-employment

Unemployment as a key policy issue

Unemployment is a key policy issue for supranational organisations, for national, regional and local governments and their partners, such as Training and Enterprise Councils (TECs) and Local Enterprise Companies (LECs), as well as for the individuals concerned. Indeed, the rise and persistence of high levels of unemployment in the European Union (EU) has been given prominence as:

> The single most serious challenge facing member states today. (Commission of the European Communities, 1993)

In a similar vein, a main objective of the New Labour government in Britain is to "attack unemployment"; in a speech in June 1997 Prime Minister Tony Blair announced that: the "greatest challenge" facing his government was to "bring the new workless class back into society and into useful work." (Blair, 1997, quoted in Finn, 1997).

Mass unemployment represents an enormous economic and social cost (Townsend, 1997). It has been identified as a major cause of low income and an important factor fuelling inequality in the UK – particularly during the 1980s (Goodman and Webb, 1994) and in an EU-wide review households headed by unemployed persons were highlighted as particularly at risk of poverty in all member states (Ramprakash, 1994). Indeed, it is contended that unemployment is the principal cause of social exclusion in Europe (European Anti-Poverty Network, 1997).

A wide variety of labour market programmes and changes in social security systems introduced in attempts to deal with persistent unemployment further underlines the salience of unemployment from a policy perspective. The vast majority of policy responses aimed at tackling unemployment (particularly long-term unemployment) have focused on the 'supply-side' of the labour market (that is, on actual and potential workers) – with initiatives to enhance motivation and improve job search skills, and training and retraining schemes to address deficiencies in human capital, well to the fore. In contrast, the 'demand-side' (jobs) – and specifically spatial variation/factors – has tended to be overlooked. Yet a cross-sectional study using individual- and area-level data from the 1991 Census of Population established that:

> A person's work chances are affected not just by who they are, but *where* they are. (Fieldhouse, 1996, emphasis added)

'New landscapes' of employment: implications for unemployment and non-employment

> ... decline is visible: obsolete industrial plants have been boarded up, empty warehouses are padlocked, manufacturers' names hang like broken branches from their fixings. The boards that once advertised vacancies outside the factory gates are blank, and weeds grow among the bricks and mortar and concrete platforms that launched their goods to the four corners of the world. (Danziger, 1996, p 27, describing Leicester)

The M4 corridor, running west from London to Newbury, ... fostered a myriad of small computer companies, as *did* the college-backed hothouse environment of Cambridge. (Bowen, 1990, p 142)

The labour market is the main field of interplay between economic, social and demographic systems (Blotevogel and King, 1996); it is where changes in the economic environment, social trends and demographic developments come together to create a 'new landscape' of employment and unemployment. The two quotes selected to introduce this section emphasise the juxtaposition of *decline* and *growth* in this 'new landscape', key characteristics of which include:

- *The demise of jobs in manufacturing and the growth of employment in services:* across the UK over 1.7 million jobs were lost in manufacturing in the 1970s and there was a further 1.3 million decline in the 1980s. Having accounted for nearly a third of total employment in 1971, by the mid-1990s less than 17% of all jobs were in manufacturing. At the regional and local scale the degree of employment contraction in some areas was even greater (as outlined in Chapter 5). Employment in primary industries has also been in long-term decline. While jobs have been lost in primary and manufacturing industries there has been an expansion of employment in services. The rate of expansion has been particularly pronounced in business and miscellaneous services, with a net increase of about 2 million jobs between 1981 and 1996 (IER, 1996).

- *A reduced demand for traditional skilled manual labour – predominantly men:* changes in patterns of industrial employment have resulted in a dramatic reduction in demand for many skills associated with the production of the output of these industries. In particular, the numbers employed in skilled craft trades have declined by 0.9 million between 1981 and the mid-1990s (IER, 1996). Many of these were full-time jobs, traditionally filled by men. A further factor contributing to the reduction in demand for these skills is changes in the way work is organised within industries, with a general shift from manual in favour of non-manual occupations across the occupational spectrum.

- *A greater premium on higher level skills/ qualifications –* and concomitantly, *a reduction in employment opportunities for those with no/few formal qualifications:* over the last two decades there has been an important expansion of employment in managerial and administrative, professional and associated occupations: between 1981 and the mid-1990s there was a net gain of 2.7 million jobs in these occupations. The highly qualified are concentrated within these occupational groups. Indeed, across much of the rest of the occupational spectrum the demand for formal educational qualifications has increased, and there has been a marked reduction in employment opportunities for those with few/no qualifications (Nickell and Bell, 1995). In 1996 there were about 0.8 million fewer people employed in other (unskilled) occupations than in 1981 (IER, 1996).

- *A growth in 'flexible' working and labour market insecurity:* alongside a decline in the number of full-time permanent jobs, there has been an increase in part-time employment, self-employment and temporary working. The increase in part-time employment has been most prominent: with a net gain of over 1.7 million part-time jobs over the period from 1981 to the mid-1990s. Growth in all of these forms of employment is part of a more general trend towards greater 'flexibility' in working arrangements (Beatson, 1995; Meadows, 1996). The use of terms such as 'uncertain', 'precarious', 'deformalised' and 'deregularised' as descriptors of these employment relationships (Green, 1997) is indicative of the perceived labour market insecurity associated with many of these employment forms. Traditionally, the vast majority of individuals in 'flexible' employment were women, but increasing numbers of men are now working flexibly.

- *A greater number of women in employment:* in the mid-1990s women accounted for about half of all those in employment, compared with less than one third 40 years previously. There has been an increase in the number of women seeking employment over this period – particularly married women (McRae, 1997). Changes in both the industrial and occupational structure of employment have favoured women. In simplistic terms, therefore, in the 'new landscapes' of employment women emerge as the 'gainers' and men as the 'losers'.

Of particular significance for the present study is a further feature of the 'new landscape':

- *The entrenchment of high levels of unemployment and of non-participation* – particularly among *some sub-groups* of the population (notably older men) and in *some areas* (notably parts of the larger cities in northern Britain and in inner London): it is these high levels of unemployment and non-employment – and their spatial manifestations – that form the focus for examination in Chapter 4.

The development of this 'new landscape' of employment (and non-employment) has resulted in 'new fissures' in British society. The term '30-30-40 society' has been used to distinguish the main lines of fracture (Hutton, 1995), with distinctions being made between:

- the *30% 'disadvantaged'* – those outside employment;

- the *30% 'marginalised and insecure'* – temporary workers and part-time and full-time workers with only a short tenure (to date) in their current employment;

- the *40% 'advantaged'* – full-time and part-time workers with a longer tenure in their current job.

This report is concerned with the 'disadvantaged' and their geographical distribution. Hence, it is appropriate here to highlight the main geographical dimensions of employment and socioeconomic change more generally, and associated implications for unemployment and non-employment.

The geography of employment change

Debates on the changing geography of employment have highlighted both regional and urban–rural dimensions of change. In the British context the main regional distinctions have been captured in the phrase the 'North–South divide' (Lewis and Townsend, 1989; Smith, 1989; Regional Policy Commission, 1996) – with the more depressed areas of northern Britain (including the Northern region, the North West and Scotland) suffering greater employment losses/slower employment growth than the regions of southern England (including East Anglia, the South West and the South East [outside London]). Although there have been variations in the size of these interregional differentials over time – with the early 1990s being marked by a convergence in regional fortunes (Martin, 1993) – reference is still made to the 'North–South divide'. Other regional divisions exist: for example, an 'East–West' divide – with the more eastern regions facing towards Europe tending to fare on some economic indicators somewhat better than those of western Britain. However, much greater attention has been paid to *intraregional* divisions.

Although some reference is made in subsequent chapters to interregional variations, the main focus of this study is on other geographical dimensions of variation. Within Britain there are significant *urban–rural* distinctions in employment change (Fothergill and Gudgin, 1982; Townsend, 1993) – with the greatest job losses in the largest cities (as outlined in Chapter 6) and job gains in smaller towns and rural areas. This is part of a more general trend of 'decentralisation' of employment and population.

To date, concerns about 'decentralisation' and the deterioration in the economic fortunes and social structures of the largest cities have been more apparent in the USA than in Europe. In the 1970s and 1980s there was lagging job growth in the central areas of US cities compared to the suburbs, and America's urban poor grew more socially and economically isolated and physically concentrated in central areas in the face of declining populations, rising crime and inadequate school systems. Across the USA the poverty rate in cities rose 50% between 1970 and 1993 (US Department of Housing and Urban Development, 1997).

Economic restructuring has led to social and spatial polarisation within cities (Badcock, 1997). The term 'new urban poverty' is often used to describe poor, segregated neighbourhoods in which a substantial majority of individual adults are either unemployed or have dropped out of the labour force altogether. It is the disappearance of work from such neighbourhoods, and the consequences of that disappearance for both social and cultural life, that has been identified as the central problem of American inner-city ghettos (Wilson, 1987).

Across Europe there is a wish to avoid the worst excesses of the 'Americanisation' of European cities – through the spread, entrenchment and increasing isolation from the mainstream economy of 'urban backwater spaces' (Kunzmann, 1996) – characterised by spatial concentrations of the long-term jobless. In an attempt to counter such trends there is a new policy emphasis on 'urban areas in difficulty', thus underlining the salience of the urban focus of this study.

Measuring unemployment and non-employment

Conceptual issues in measuring unemployment and non-employment

As highlighted in Chapter 2, there is widespread policy and academic concern about the persistence of high levels of unemployment, and the uneven distribution of unemployment between population sub-groups and areas. Unemployment is one of the most widely quoted socioeconomic indicators. From an 'economic' perspective it is used variously as an indicator of labour market imbalance, of economic performance, and as a device for ranking areas for policy assistance. From a 'social' perspective it is used as an indicator of deprivation and social distress. Yet the task of defining and measuring unemployment in a clear and non-ambiguous fashion is a problematic one.

Conventionally (according to definitions adopted in the Labour Force Survey), the adult population is divided into three main categories in labour market terms, as illustrated in Figure 1:

- the *employed*: categorised in Figure 1 as those who have a paid job in an employee or self-employed capacity, or who are on government-supported training and employment programmes, or who are unpaid family workers;

- the *unemployed*: categorised in Figure 1 as those who do not have a job but who are available to take up a job (this is the 'ILO definition' of unemployment);

- the *inactive*: all remaining members of the adult population, who may be further subdivided into those who want a job and those who do not want a job.

(The 'unemployed' and 'inactive' together constitute the *non-employed*.)

In reality, however, these distinctions are not so clear-cut. The boundaries between employment and unemployment, and between unemployment and inactivity, have been variously described as 'fuzzy', 'blurred' and 'fluid' (Bryson and McKay, 1994; Nicaise et al, 1995). Rather than neatly bounded categories, there is a continuum from 'complete employment' to 'complete non-employment', with 'unemployment' somewhere in between:

> If every person could be categorised as in work or out of work we should have no problem. There are umpteen categories in which people can be put, varying degrees of part-time work, seeking work and not seeking work. (Professor David Bartholomew, in House of Commons Employment Committee, 1996)

The ambiguities and complexities outlined above are further highlighted by the fact that unemployment is only one possible response to imbalance in the interactions between labour supply and labour demand (Owen et al, 1984). In the face of employment loss in a particular local area there may be:

- a decline in the number of people seeking work (that is, a decline in economic activity rates); and/or

- an increase in the numbers of people commuting to jobs in other areas; and/or

- net out-migration of people to other areas; as well as

- an increase in unemployment.

Figure 1: Conventional categorisation of employment, unemployment and inactivity

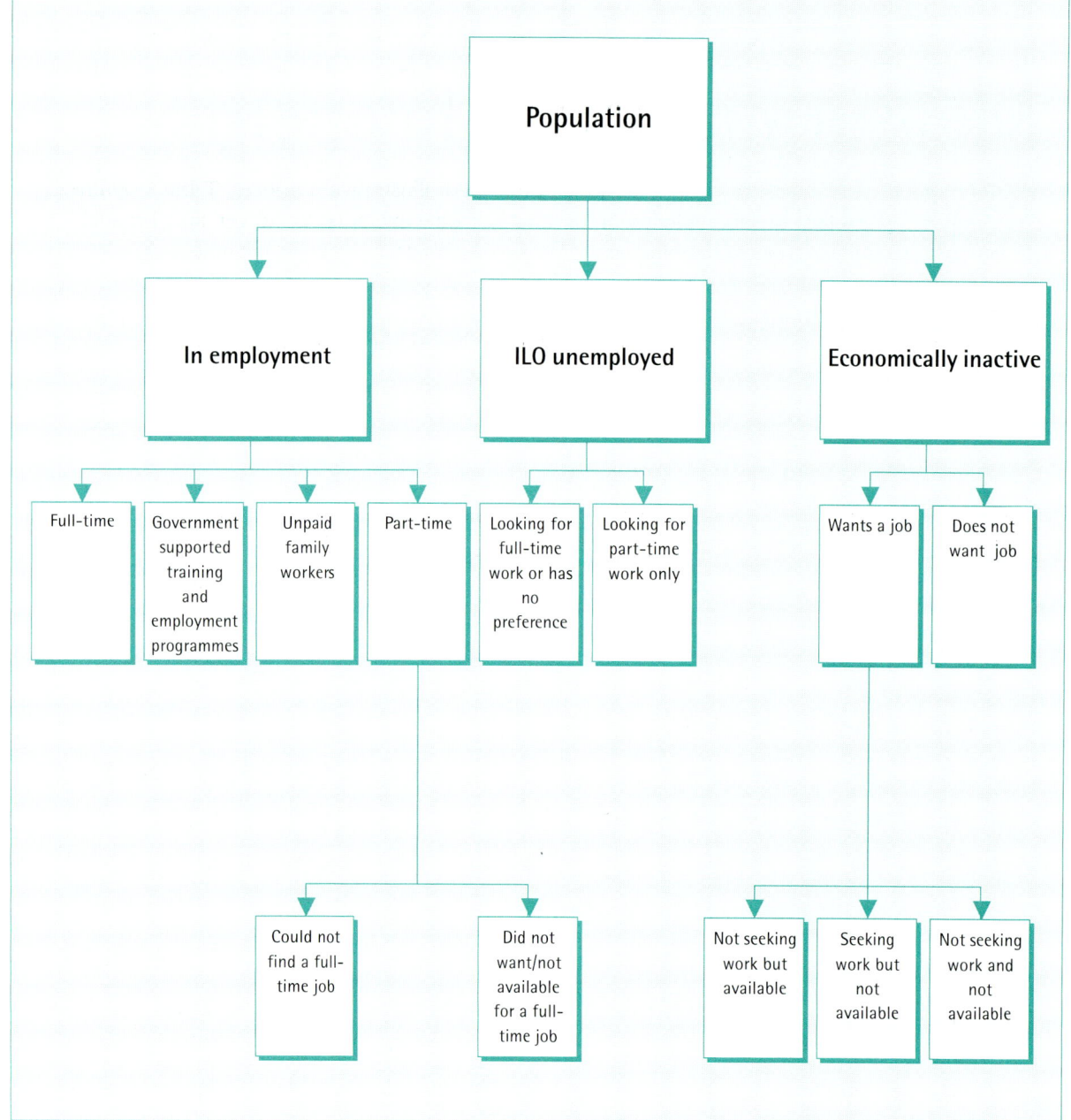

Note: The 'ILO unemployed' are people without a job who are available to start work in the next two weeks and who had either looked for work in the previous four weeks or are waiting to start a job already obtained.

ILO = International Labour Office.

Indeed, it may be the case that there is no increase in unemployment in the face of a localised employment loss. For example, a study focusing on the changing economic position of men in the coalfield areas of Britain has shown that the impact of job losses in the mining industry tended to be translated into increasing inactivity and net out-migration, rather than unemployment (Beatty and Fothergill, 1996; Beatty et al, 1997a). Hence, 'conventional' unemployment may measure only 'the tip of the ice-berg' of joblessness. Indeed, one group of researchers (Beatty et al, 1997b) has derived estimates of 'real unemployment' (encompassing groups of the 'hidden unemployed', such as those on government schemes and excess numbers of early retirees and of those suffering permanent sickness), and has shown that the level of 'real unemployment' is considerably higher than the level of 'conventional' unemployment.

Given the ambiguity of the concept of unemployment, any notion of a single 'true' measure of unemployment is likely to be flawed. Hence, there would seem to be merit in adopting a broader measure of non-employment alongside (or in place of) unemployment, or a battery of cumulative (or overlapping) measures of unemployment and non-employment. In the USA the US Bureau of Labor Statistics publishes six alternative measures of unemployment, ranging from:

- *U1:* the 'narrowest' measure – those unemployed for 15 weeks or longer; to

- *U6:* the 'broadest' measure – the total unemployed *plus* all 'marginally attached' workers (that is, those who want work and are available for work, although they are not currently seeking work) *plus* all people employed part time for economic reasons.

Hence, as well as the 'unemployed', the broadest measure includes some individuals who in a conventional categorisation would be included as 'inactive'. In the UK context the Employment Policy Institute (1996) has published alternative indicators of unemployment at the individual and household levels, while Green and Hasluck (1998) have also used the Labour Force Survey to operationalise alternative indicators of 'labour reserve' at the regional scale using data from the Labour Force Survey.

For illustrative purposes, Table 1 outlines some exemplar 'narrower' and 'broader' indicators of unemployment and non-employment. This list of indicators *U1-U9* is not intended to be definitive or exhaustive; rather it is illustrative of the range of possible indicators of unemployment and non-employment that may be of interest. The development of such measures reflects a growing recognition that in an increasingly diverse and dynamic labour market conventional measures of employment, ILO unemployment and economic inactivity are insufficient (Laux, 1997).

From a conceptual perspective, therefore, it is argued that 'unemployment' tells only 'part of the story' of joblessness. In order to get a more complete picture of changes in *how many* people, and *who* are excluded from employment *where*, it is contended that it is necessary to extend the analysis beyond unemployment to non-employment.

Table 1: Exemplar alternative indicators of unemployment and non-employment

Indicator	Definition
U1	Those unemployed for at least 12 months
U2	ILO unemployed
U3	*U2* + those employed on government-supported education and training programmes
U4	*U3* + those inactive who want a job but are not seeking work because they believe no jobs are available*
U5	*U4* + those inactive who want a job and are not seeking work† but who are available
U6	*U5* + those inactive who want a job and seeking work but who are not available
U7	*U3* + all those inactive who want a job
U8	*U7* + those part-timers who could not find a full-time job
U9	*U2* + all those inactive

Notes: * Discouraged workers (these are a subset of those who are inactive and want a job).
† For whatever reason – not just those who are discouraged workers.

Practical issues in measuring unemployment and non-employment

In addition to the conceptual difficulties regarding issues of 'definition' and 'interpretation' in the measurement of unemployment outlined above, there are a number of practical difficulties. These practical difficulties have mainly centred on the *data sources* used to measure unemployment.

When unemployment is used as an 'official' socioeconomic indicator in Great Britain, statistics are derived from one of two main data sources:

- the claimant count unemployment series; or
- the Labour Force Survey.

A third important source – often used for micro area level analyses – is:

- the Census of Population.

These three sources differ in terms of their *coverage*, the *scope of the definition* of unemployment adopted, the *basis of that definition*, the *frequency* of data collection, and (of particular importance for a study of geographical variations) the *spatial disaggregation* available (see Table 2). (Information on unemployment – adopting either similar or different definitions – is also collected in a range of local level surveys.)

What is immediately apparent from Table 2 is that there are important differences in the coverage of, and scope and basis of the definition adopted in, the alternative unemployment data sources. Given these differences it is not surprising that for a single area at a single point in time estimates of unemployment can vary quite markedly according to the data source used (Green, 1995; Sly, 1994; Woolford and Denman, 1993). Heightening awareness of such differences, along with changes made to benefit regulations and the scope of the claimant count, led throughout the 1980s and early 1990s to the levelling of various concerns about the validity of unemployment statistics, with accusations being made that the unemployment statistics were being 'fiddled', for political and administrative purposes. In the mid-1990s these concerns prompted a Royal Statistical Society review of the measurement of unemployment (Royal Statistical Society, 1995) and a House of Commons Employment Committee (1996) enquiry into unemployment and employment statistics. In these reviews claims concerning the 'fiddling' of unemployment statistics were rejected, but a much wider debate concerning the generation, presentation and dissemination of unemployment (and other labour market) statistics was opened up (for example, see Steel, 1997).

Table 2: Comparison of the main sources of unemployment data

Feature	Claimant series	Labour Force Survey	Census of Population
Coverage	All claimant unemployed	Sample survey	National census
Scope of definition	By-product of administrative system – sensitive to benefit regulations	Without a job, available to start work within two weeks, looked for work in last four weeks, or waiting to start job*	Unemployed in week prior to census and looking for job, or waiting to start work already accepted
Basis of definition	Administrative regulations	Interviewer applying ILO definition	Self-enumeration
Spatial disaggregations	Wards, postcode sectors	TECs/LECs, large local authority districts, counties, unitary authorities	Enumeration districts and census wards
Frequency	Monthly	Quarterly	Decennial

Note: * Various alternative definitions are possible using the Labour Force Survey – the one listed here is the most commonly used ILO definition.

So far, attention has been concentrated on unemployment *counts* – which may be used to measure the changing absolute *level* of unemployment. However, in order to facilitate comparisons between areas which differ in size it is usual to calculate the relative extent (or incidence) of unemployment by using an unemployment *rate*. Here it is appropriate to introduce some of the most widely used labour market 'rates', which are used in the empirical analyses in subsequent chapters. First, the crucial measure of participation in the labour market is:

- the *economic activity rate*: the economically active population (that is, those in employment plus the unemployed) expressed as a percentage of the total population of interest. (This may be defined variously according to purpose, for example, all adults, adults of working age, men aged 25-44, etc.)

The converse of this is:

- the *inactivity rate*: the economically inactive population expressed as a percentage of the total population of interest.

However, perhaps the best known of the commonly used measures is:

- the *unemployment rate*: conventionally defined as the unemployed population expressed as a percentage of the economically active population.

The other 'rate' which is a major focus of attention in this study is:

- the *non-employment rate*: the unemployed plus the inactive as a percentage of the population, which may be interpreted as a measure of 'complete joblessness'.

In this report reference is made to all of the 'rates' identified above and all three of the data sources referred to in Table 2. From a practical perspective it is important to note that while 'counts' may be readily available at a local scale, the derivation of rates is often more problematic (Turok, 1997).

Geographical issues

A range of geographical units are used in presentation of the analyses in subsequent chapters (for further details of these units, and associated geographical classifications see Appendix A). In descending order of size the levels for which data are presented are:

- *National:* the main focus here is on *Great Britain*.

- *Regional:* the *standard statistical regions* are the main focus of interest here, although reference is also made to a slightly more detailed classification in which a distinction is made between *metropolitan counties* and *regional remainders*.

- *Local:* here three different sets of geographical units are referred to:

  – local labour market areas (LLMAs);

  – travel-to-work areas (TTWAs);

  – local authority districts (LADs).

  LLMAs and TTWAs are 'functional' areas, defined using data on commuting to work flows, such that the majority of residents work in the local area *and* the majority of jobs in the area are filled by local residents. By contrast, LADs are 'administrative' areas. Since there are 280 LLMAs, 322 TTWAs and 459 LADs in Great Britain for the analyses presented in subsequent chapters use is made of *classifications* of these local areas – in order to summarise and compare trends for different types of areas (for further details see Appendix A).

- *Micro areas:* this term is used to refer to analysis at the *ward* level.

Since it is not possible in this study to examine patterns and trends in unemployment and non-employment in all parts of Britain at all scales, particular attention in the more detailed analyses is focused on three contrasting urban areas:

- Merseyside;

- the West Midlands conurbation;

- London – notably Inner London.

('Merseyside and the 'West Midlands' are used to refer to the former metropolitan county areas.)

4

Inter- and intra-urban variations in unemployment and non-employment

Introduction

The purpose of this chapter is to use information from each of the three data sources identified in Chapter 3, pp 10-11 to provide 'snapshot' information on the geographical distribution of *stocks* of unemployment and non-employment at different points in time. Those analyses based on Census of Population data are restricted to 1991 (and comparisons with 1981), while for analyses using other data sources more up-to-date information (up to the mid-1990s) is used. Patterns and trends at the national and regional scales are examined (see below), before the focus of attention shifts to the local and micro area scales (p 20).

The analyses presented show how the incidence of unemployment and non-employment varies over time and space, with a particular focus on:

- *where* the unemployed and non-employed are; and

- *whether*, and *where*, they have become more (or less) concentrated geographically.

Since the development of 'new landscapes' of employment have favoured some groups more than others, for the most part the analyses presented are disaggregated by population sub-group – with the experience of men being distinguished from that of women, and with some further disaggregation by age group.

Overview at national and regional scales

The national picture

Using the ILO definition of *unemployment*, Figure 2 shows how the overall level of unemployment in Great Britain fell from a level of approximately 3 million in the mid-1980s to less than 2 million in 1990, before rising again to over 2.8 million in 1993. Thereafter, the unemployment level declined steadily once again. Throughout this period the level and incidence (see Figure 3) of unemployment for men exceeded that for women.

Turning to *inactivity rates* for Great Britain over the same period, cyclical variations are less pronounced. For men of working age (16-64 years) the general trend is one of increase: from 1984 to 1990 approximately 12% in this group were inactive, but from 1990 onwards the rate increased steadily to over 15% in 1996 (see Figure 4). Inactivity rates are highest in the youngest (16-24 years) and oldest (50-64 years) age groups, but the most significant feature to emerge from Figure 4 is the *upward trend in the inactivity rate for men in all age groups since 1990*. By 1996, 7% of men aged 25-49 years and 28% of those aged 50-64 were inactive.

Conversely, for women of working age (see Figure 5) the general trend is one of *decreasing* inactivity rates (although the incidence of inactivity remains higher among women than among men). The main decreases in inactivity are among women aged 35 and over (as for men there has been a marked increase in inactivity in the youngest age group – reflecting the rise in 'staying on' rates in full-time education).

Figure 2: ILO unemployment levels by gender, Great Britain (1984-96)

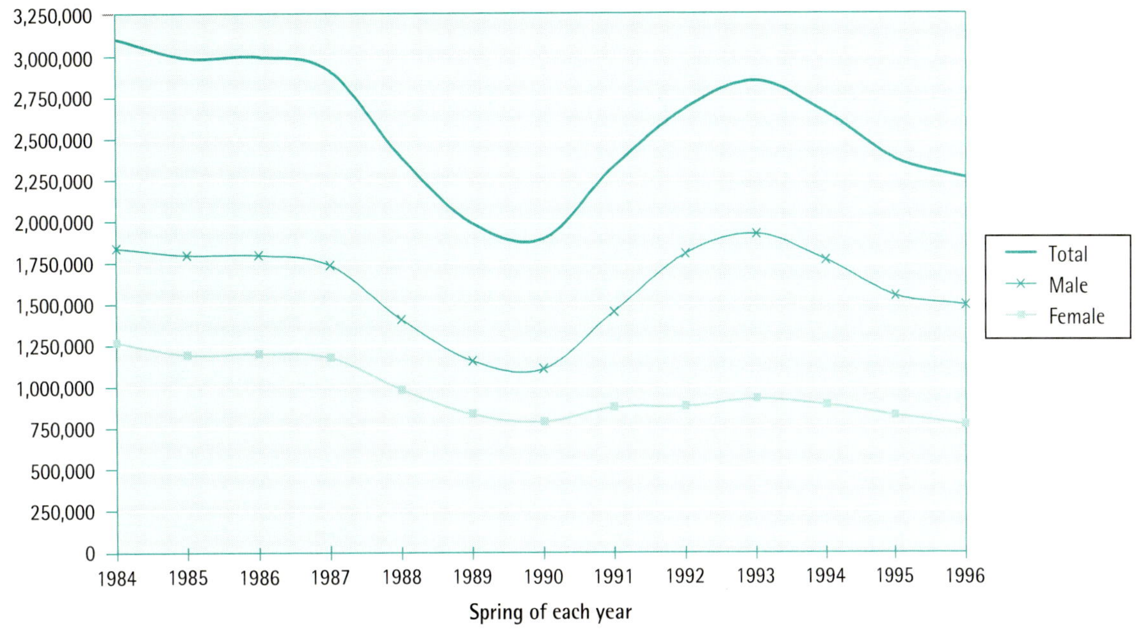

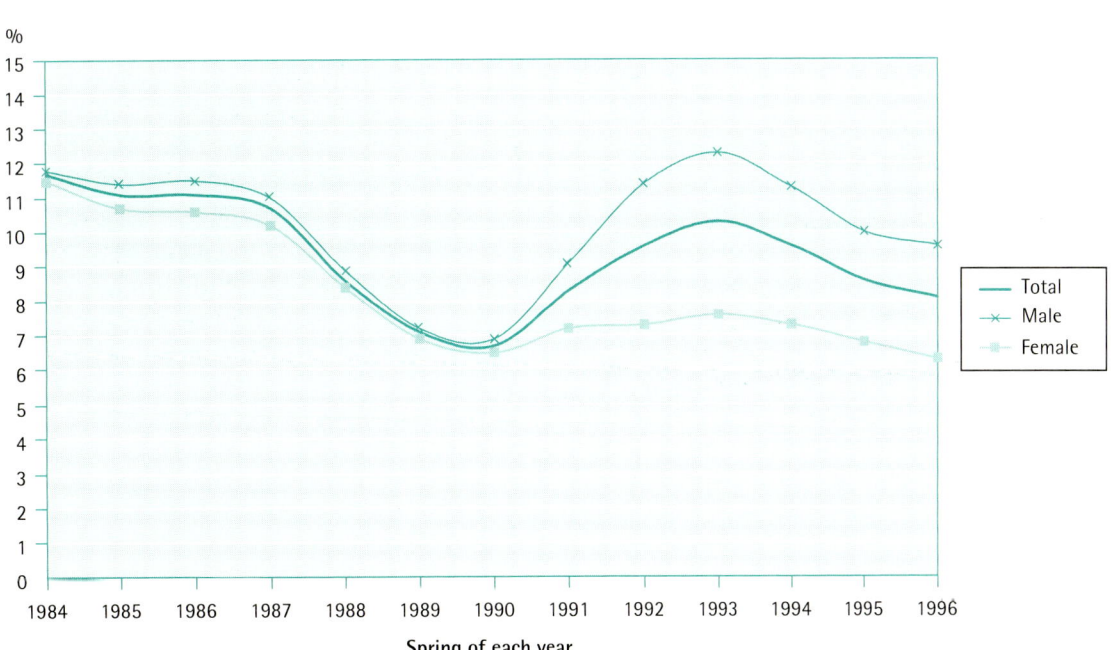

Source: *Labour Force Survey*

Figure 3: ILO unemployment rates by gender, Great Britain (1984-96)

Source: *Labour Force Survey*

Together, the unemployed and inactive constitute the *non-employed*. The trend in the non-employment rate for men shows some of the cyclical fluctuations evident in the unemployment rate (see Figure 6). Hence the proportion of men of working age non-employed declined from 22% in the mid-1980s to 18% in 1990, before increasing to 25% in 1993, before falling again to less than 24% in 1995-96 as the economy recovered. These cyclical fluctuations are much less marked for women of working age: for this sub-group the non-employment rate declined from over 40% in 1984-85 to 33% in 1990, and thereafter the proportion has remained relatively constant.

Figure 4: Inactivity rates for men by age group, Great Britain (1984-96)

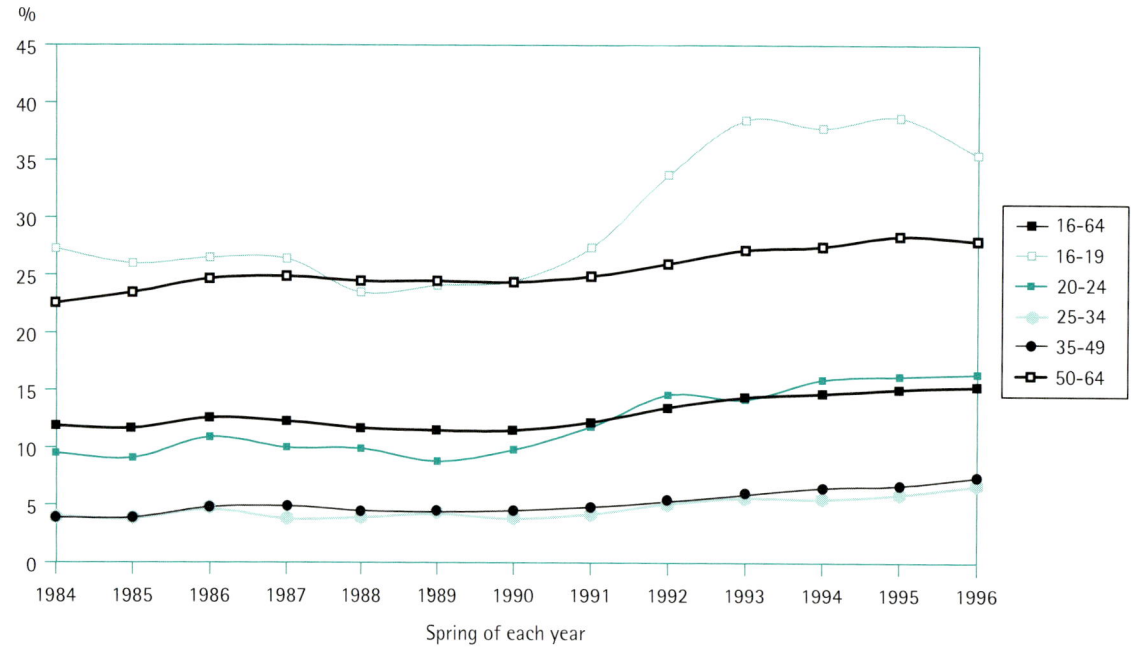

Source: Labour Force Survey

Figure 5: Inactivity rates for women by age group, Great Britain (1984-96)

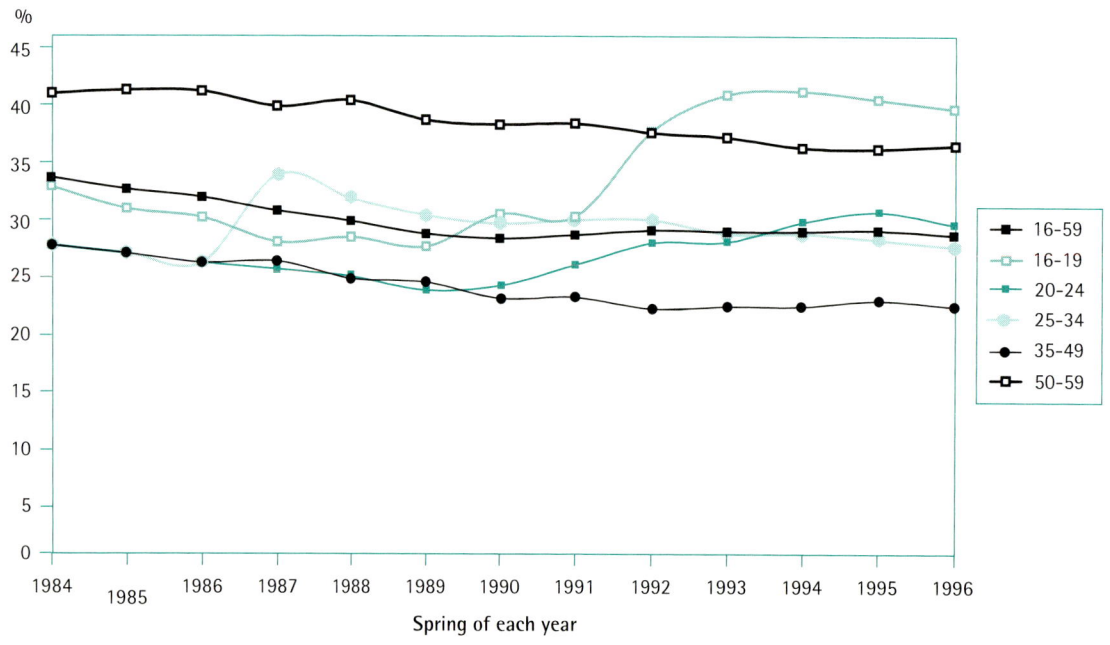

Source: Labour Force Survey

The analyses presented in the remainder of the report focus mainly on the problems of men, on the basis that the general trend in non-employment for men of working age is one of increase, while the non-employment trend for women of working age is one of decrease. Nevertheless, it is important to remember that some groups of women face particular disadvantage in the labour market, in terms of suffering higher levels of unemployment and inactivity, as well as a disproportionate concentration in part-time and low paid jobs (May, 1997). Moreover, as for men, so for women there are spatial variations in the extent of labour market disadvantage, and since women are particularly reliant on 'local' job opportunities relative to men, they may suffer particularly in the face of localised job losses.

The regional picture

Of course, the national level picture outlined above disguises important variations in experience at the regional level. Concentrating on men, Figures 7 and 8 show ILO unemployment rates and non-employment rates, respectively, indexed to the Great Britain rates over the period from 1984 to 1996 (for ease of presentation Southern and Midlands regions are shown on separate charts from Northern Britain and Wales).

Figure 6: Non-employment rates for working age population by gender, Great Britain (1984-96)

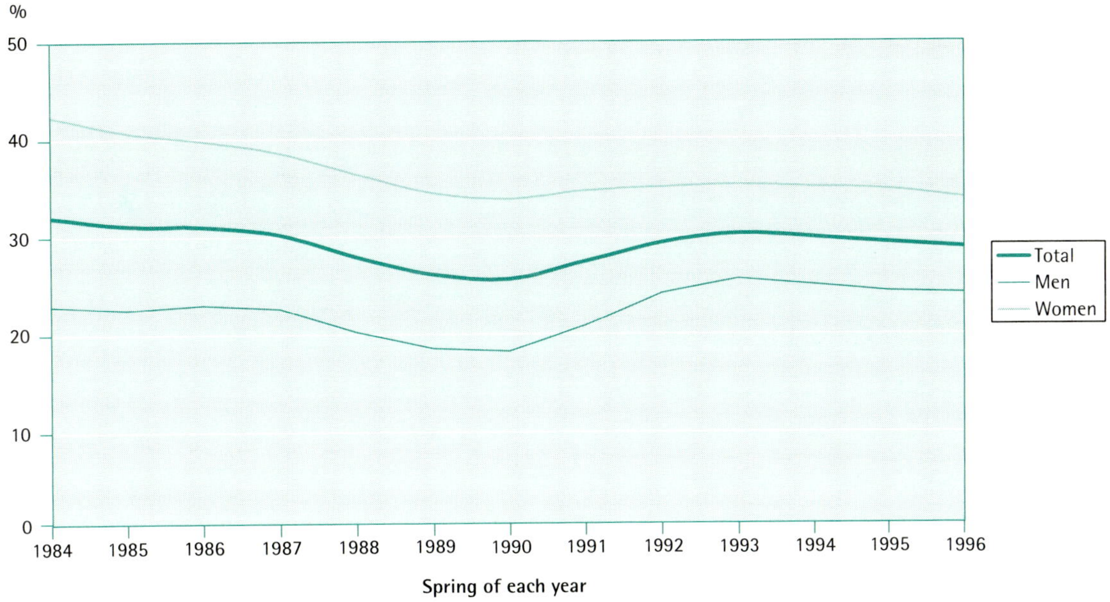

Source: Labour Force Survey

Figure 7: Indices of ILO unemployment rates for men by region (1984-96)
(a) Southern and Midlands regions

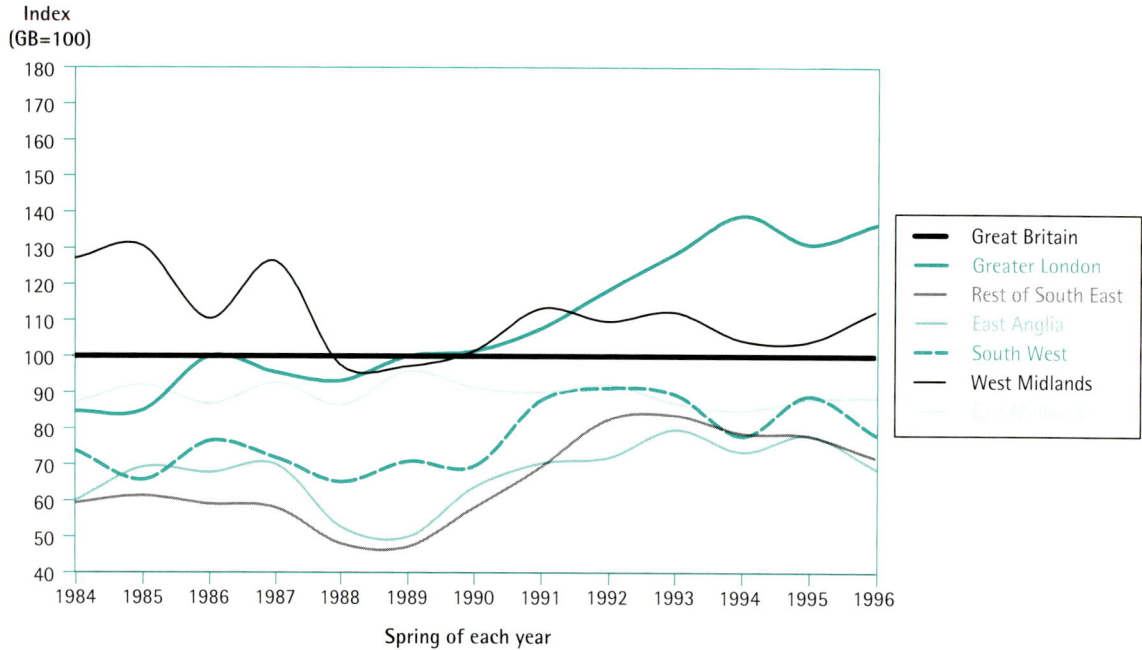

Source: Labour Force Survey

(b) Northern Britain and Wales

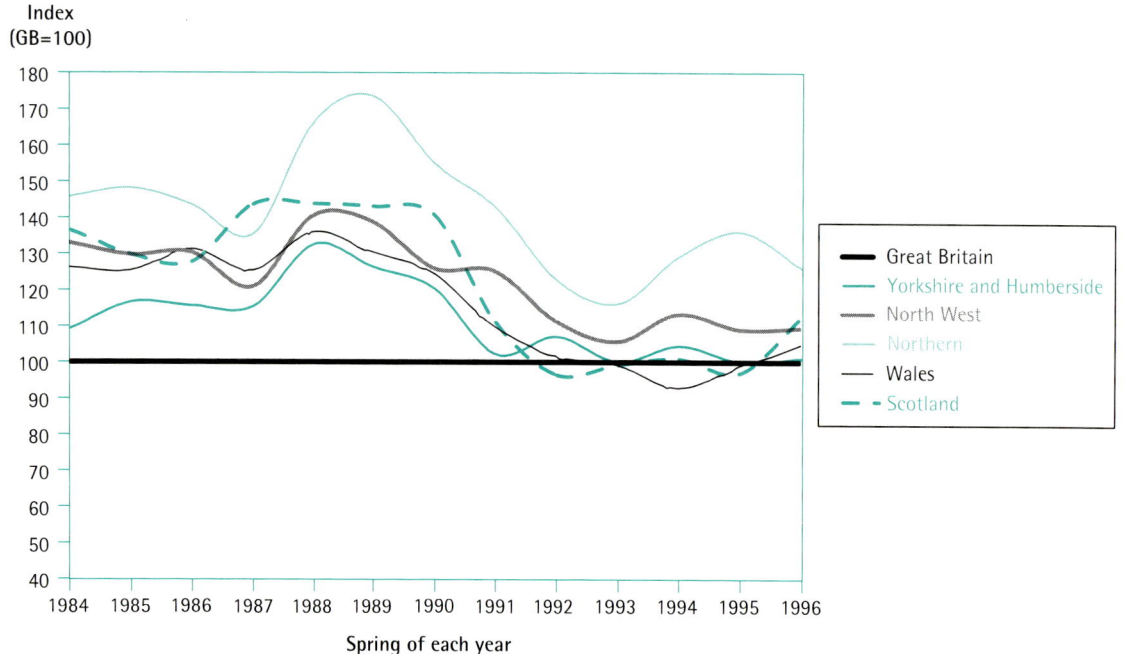

Source: Labour Force Survey

Figure 8: Indices of non-employment rates for men by region (1984-96)
(a) Southern and Midlands regions

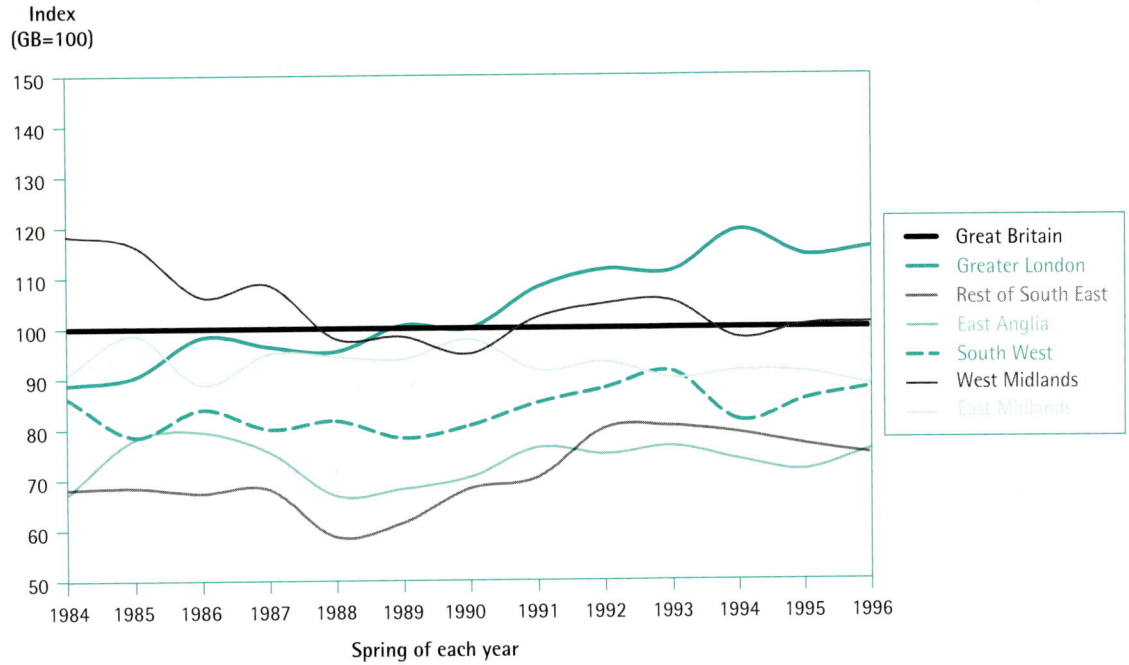

Source: Labour Force Survey

(b) Northern Britain and Wales

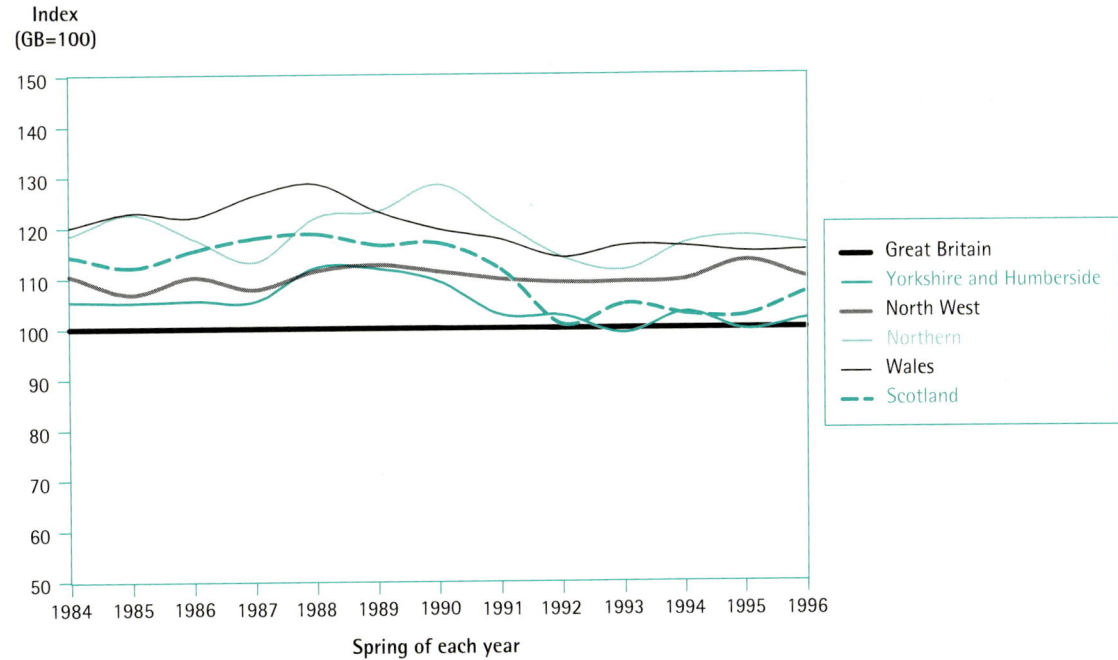

Source: Labour Force Survey

Figure 9: Indices of inactivity rates for men by region (1984-96)
(a) Southern and Midlands regions

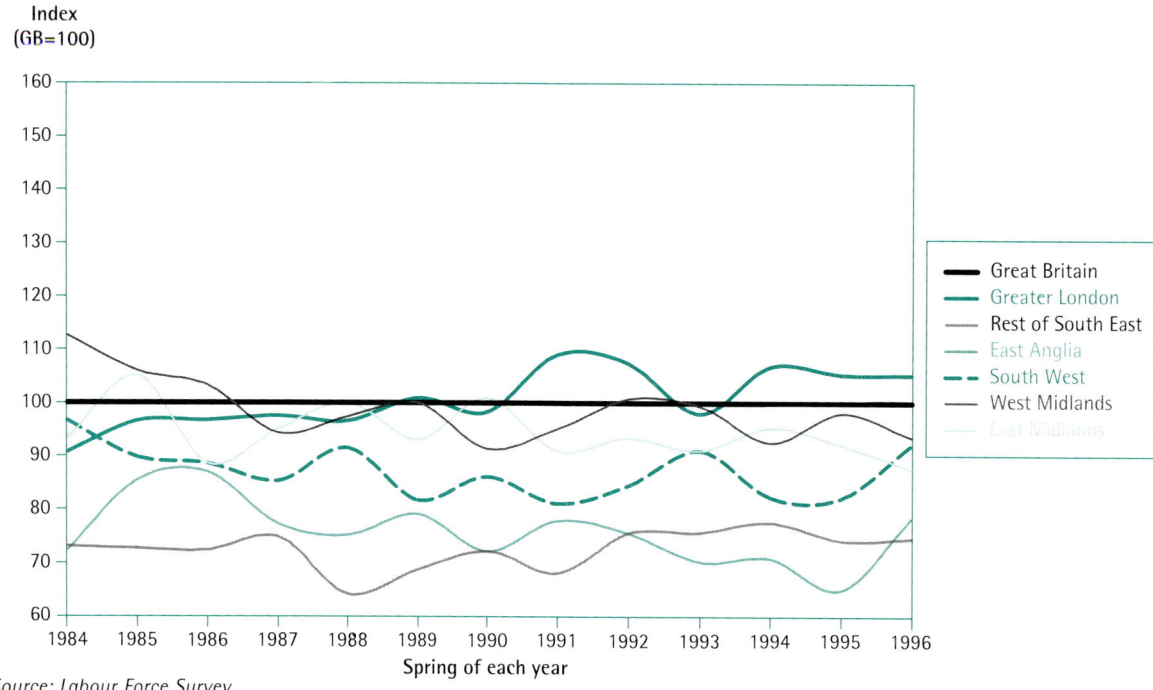

Source: Labour Force Survey

(b) Northern Britain and Wales

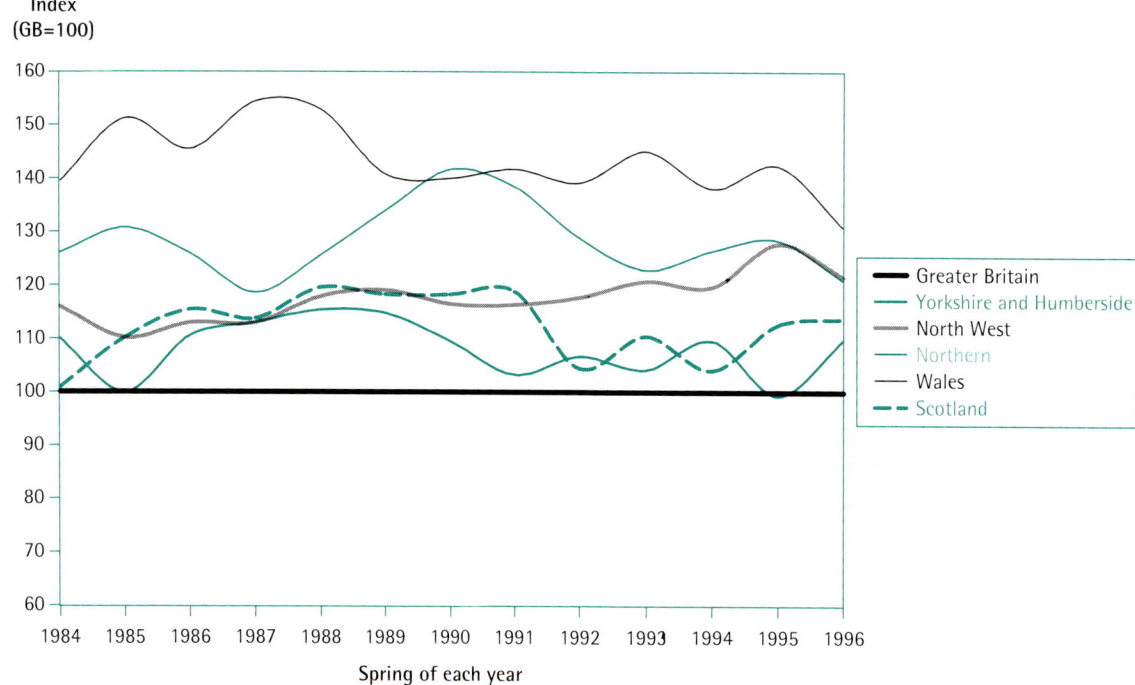

Source: Labour Force Survey

On the *ILO unemployment rate* the main features emerging are:

- Lower than average unemployment rates for men throughout the period in the *Rest of the South East, East Anglia*, the *South West* and the *East Midlands*. Some convergence towards the Great Britain average is evident in the early 1990s, but in most cases some divergence is evident towards the end of the

period. For women there is a similar general picture of a lower than average incidence of unemployment, but regional differentials are generally less pronounced than is the case for men.

- Generally higher than average unemployment rates for men throughout the period in the *Northern region*, the *North West, Wales, Scotland, Yorkshire and*

Humberside and the *West Midlands*. The Northern region consistently displays the highest unemployment rates in Great Britain. In general, the trend is one of convergence towards the national average in the early 1990s – indeed, in Scotland and Wales the unemployment rate for men fell below the average for Great Britain. The West Midlands is the most distinctive region in this group: in 1988 and 1989 the regional unemployment rate fell below the national level (as in other 'Southern' and 'Midlands' regions). For women, as for men, unemployment rates are generally below the national average in this group of regions.

- *Greater London* is distinctive in that it displays a below average unemployment rate throughout much of the 1980s, and then an incidence of unemployment in excess of the national average in the 1990s. The picture is one of a relative deterioration in 'performance' – with a steady increase in unemployment relative to the national trend (for women as well as men).

On the *non-employment rate* the general patterns of national:regional variation are similar, with a lower than average incidence of non-employment in the *Rest of the South East*, *East Anglia*, the *South West* and the *East Midlands*, and a higher than average incidence of non-employment in the *Northern region*, the *North West*, *Wales*, *Scotland*, *Yorkshire and Humberside* and the *West Midlands*. As previously, the trend in Greater London is one of relative deterioration compared with the national average. Once again, the same general picture of regional:national differentials is evident for men and women, although the size of the differentials is greater in the case of men than of women of working age. However, there is some evidence that:

- any trend towards regional convergence in *non-employment* is less marked than for *unemployment*.

This suggests that the trend in *inactivity* (the non-employed comprise the unemployed plus the inactive) is *not* one of convergence. Inactivity rates, therefore, must be disproportionately higher in traditionally 'high unemployment' regions than traditionally 'low unemployment' regions. As Figure 9 shows, this is, in fact, the case. Wales and the Northern region display the highest inactivity rates for men of working age

throughout the period, and in the North West the inactivity rate diverges from the national average over the period. In contrast, the rest of the South East and East Anglia have the lowest inactivity rates. The deterioration in the fortunes of Greater London relative to the national average situation is also evident on this measure.

Turning to the *three major urban areas* selected for more detailed analysis, Table 3 shows the proportion of men *not working* by broad age group (excluding those in age groups at the extremes of the working age spectrum) in:

- *1979:* before the onset of mass unemployment in the 1980s;
- *1986:* the mid-1980s peak in the non-employment rate for men of working age;
- *1990:* at the end of the late 1980s boom;
- *1993:* when unemployment peaked at the national level following the early 1990s recession;
- *1995:* as the economic situation improved.

Although there is some variation in the shares of men not working in the three urban areas – with Merseyside displaying the highest rate of non-employment throughout the period – there are also some important common features evident across all three areas:

- There was a massive increase in levels of non-employment for men in the first part of the 1980s – in 1986 over one quarter of men in Merseyside aged 25-44 years were not working, while in the 25-44 years age group the comparative proportion was nearly one third. In Greater London the shares not working more than doubled, while in the West Midlands Metropolitan County there was a three-fold increase in the incidence of not working.

- Despite a reduction in the proportions not working in the late 1980s economic recovery, the numbers of men without work remained stubbornly above the pre-1980s recession levels.

- In 1993 levels of non-employment were at least as high as, or higher than, in 1986. This increase in non-employment was particularly pronounced in Greater London.

- Despite a reduction in unemployment rates post-1993, decreases in non-employment are not particularly marked (and are not apparent at all in Merseyside).

Table 3: Proportion of men not working in three large urban areas (%)

Age group	1979	1986	1990	1993	1995
Merseyside					
25–44 years	13.8	26.9	15.9	25.7	26.4
45–59 years	18.4	32.0	25.0	34.6	34.8
West Midlands Metropolitan County					
25–44 years	6.6	18.6	12.4	19.6	18.7
45–59 years	8.1	24.3	19.3	28.4	27.4
Greater London					
25–44 years	6.9	15.8	11.3	21.0	19.0
45–59 years	6.8	15.6	13.9	26.0	23.8

Source: Labour Force Survey

Aside from the youngest working age groups where the increase in 'staying on' rates in full-time education is contributing to rising non-employment rates, it is in the oldest age groups that the increase in non-employment is most pronounced. In the three main urban areas selected for particular investigation in this study it is in Merseyside that high levels of non-employment are most entrenched. Figure 10 shows changes in unemployment rates and non-employment rates among men in Merseyside over the period from 1977 to 1995, illustrating the inexorable upward trend in non-employment rates – to approximately 30% for men aged 50-54 years, in excess of 40% for men aged 55-59 years and about 60% for men aged 60-64 years. There is a growing gap between unemployment and non-employment rates.

Local level variations

Introduction

As indicated in Chapter 3, p 10, the Census of Population is the most comprehensive source of socioeconomic information (including unemployment, inactivity and non-employment) on the population of Great Britain, having complete population and geographical coverage (in contrast to data sets such as the Labour Force Survey). The main drawback of the Census of Population is that it is taken only on a decennial basis. Nevertheless, it is useful in providing an overview of changes over a decade in various phenomena at a range of geographical scales. However, the calculation of change between two Censuses is not straightforward, due to changes between Censuses in the variable definitions used, the boundaries of the geographical units for which data are reported, and the definition of the resident population (see Appendix B for details of the derivation of estimates of intercensal change).

The travel-to-work area picture

At the TTWA scale, only 39 out of 322 TTWAs displayed an increase in the percentage of the population of working age not in employment over the decade from 1981 to 1991. Table 4 lists those TTWAs which exhibited an increase in the non-employment rate for those of working age of at least 1 percentage point over the decade. The list includes TTWAs based on some of the largest cities in Britain (including London, Liverpool, Glasgow and Sheffield) as well as some former mining areas (such as Cumnock and Sanquhar [Scotland], Barnsley, Mansfield and

Table 4: Unemployment and non-employment rates for persons of working age for TTWAs with largest increases in non-employment (1981-91) (%)

TTWA	Unemployment rate (1981)	Unemployment rate (1991)	Non-employment rate (1981)	Non-employment rate (1991)	Change in non-employment rate (1981-91)
Cumnock and Sanquhar	16.0	17.2	38.7	41.5	2.9
London	9.2	12.4	29.1	31.9	2.8
Liverpool	18.0	17.9	37.7	40.4	2.7
Aberdare	15.2	15.4	40.7	43.3	2.6
Barnsley	10.2	12.7	33.5	36.1	2.6
Mansfield	7.9	10.9	32.3	34.6	2.4
Oldham	11.6	11.1	28.6	30.2	1.7
Merthyr and Rhymney	15.9	13.9	40.5	42.0	1.5
Glasgow	16.1	14.7	35.4	36.9	1.5
Doncaster	11.7	12.8	35.2	36.6	1.4
Pendle	10.2	8.4	28.7	29.9	1.2
Rotherham and Mexborough	12.7	13.2	35.6	36.8	1.1
Sheffield	10.8	12.3	31.0	32.1	1.1
Sunderland	15.1	14.0	37.2	38.2	1.0

Note: All percentages are expressed to one decimal place.

Source: Census of Population

Merthyr and Rhymney). All 322 TTWAs saw a decrease in the proportion of women non-employed between 1981 and 1991, although the reduction was only 1 percentage point or less in Liverpool, Oldham and London. Hence, it was the increase in non-employment among men of working age which contributed to the overall rise in non-employment among persons of working age in the TTWAs listed in Table 4.

Table 5 lists the 12 TTWAs with the largest percentage point increases in the non-employment rate for men of working age. The largest cities are excluded from this list, although many of them did see marked increases in non-employment over the decade from 1981. Instead, the list is headed by areas which saw large localised employment losses during the period – particularly job losses associated with the run down of the coalmining industry. In Aberdare (South Wales) and Barnsley (South Yorkshire) the number of men of working age non-employed increased by 10 percentage points over the decade to 1991.

However, in these same two areas the increase in non-employment for men aged 45-59 years was 20 percentage points.

The local authority district picture

Table 6 presents similar information at the LAD scale for those LADs which exhibited an increase in non-employment of at least 4 percentage points over the decade to 1991. Excluded from this list are some LADs in South Wales where the non-employment rate in 1991 exceeded 40% (such as Rhondda, Merthyr Tydfil and Cynon Valley), which had somewhat smaller percentage point increases in the proportion of persons of working age non-employed from a higher initial base in 1981. Of 459 LADs, only 20 – the majority of which are London boroughs or large cities in northern Britain (such as Manchester, Liverpool and Glasgow) – saw a decrease in the non-employment rate for women of working age over the decade from 1981.

Figure 10: Unemployment and non-employment rates among older men in Merseyside (1977-95)
(a) Men aged 50-54 years

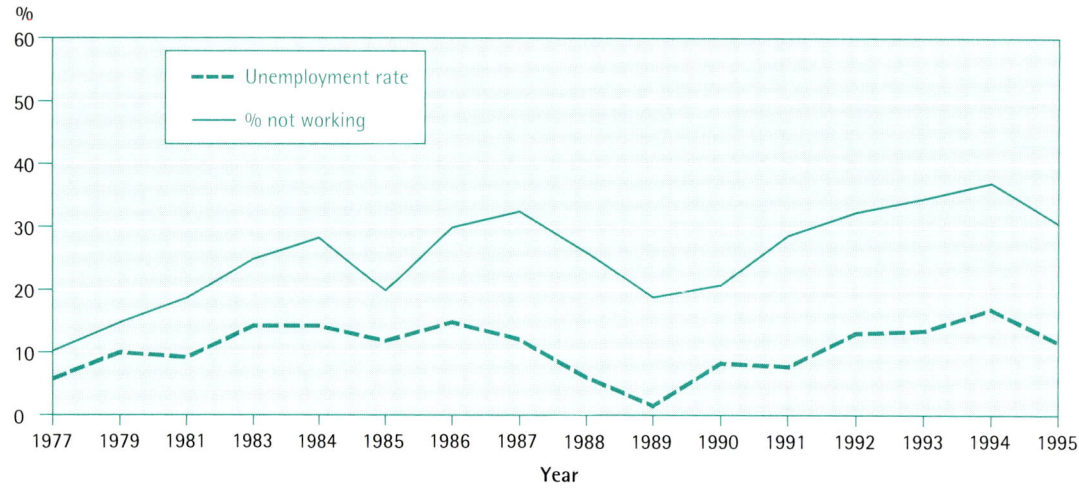

(b) Men aged 55-59 years

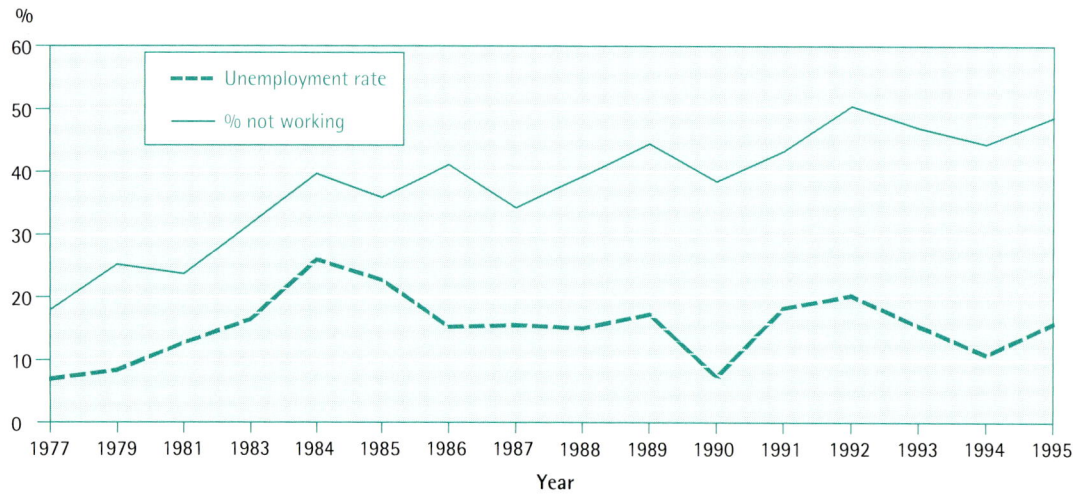

(c) Men aged 60-64 years

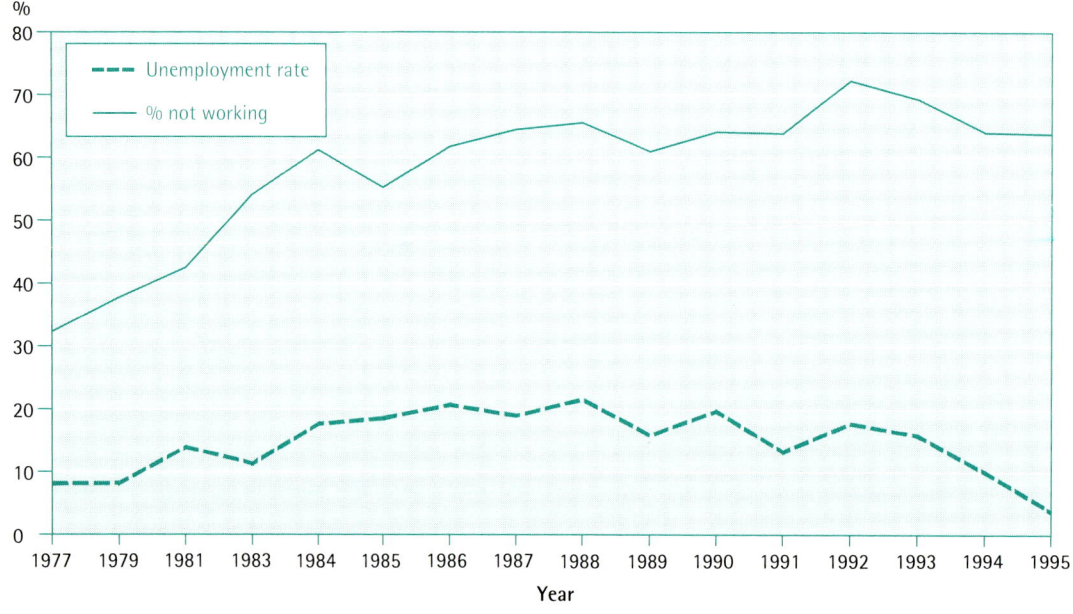

Source: Labour Force Survey

Table 5: Unemployment and non-employment rates for men of working age for TTWAs with largest increases in non-employment (1981-91) (%)

TTWA	Unemployment rate (1981)	Unemployment rate (1991)	Non-employment rate (1981)	Non-employment rate (1991)	Change in non-employment rate (1981-91)
Aberdare	16.7	19.7	28.7	39.1	10.3
Mansfield	8.8	13.4	18.8	28.7	9.9
Invergordon and Dingwall	6.4	11.3	12.2	21.8	9.6
Barnsley	11.8	16.1	22.0	31.4	9.4
South Pembrokeshire	11.9	14.5	21.4	30.0	8.6
Doncaster	12.8	15.7	21.9	30.0	8.2
Cumnock and Sanquhar	18.8	21.2	27.7	35.6	7.9
Haverfordwest	11.2	13.5	19.9	27.7	7.8
Morpeth and Ashington	11.0	14.0	21.8	29.5	7.7
Rotherham and Mexborough	14.5	16.6	23.5	31.1	7.6
Merthyr and Rhymney	17.5	17.5	29.5	37.0	7.4
Worksop	11.2	13.3	20.2	27.7	7.4

Note: All percentages are expressed to one decimal place.

Source: Census of Population

Table 6: Unemployment and non-employment rates for persons of working age for LADs with largest increases in non-employment (1981-91) (%)

TTWA	Unemployment rate (1981)	Unemployment rate (1991)	Non-employment rate (1981)	Non-employment rate (1991)	Percentage point change in non-employment rate (1981-91)
Tower Hamlets	16.1	22.3	34.8	45.0	10.2
Newham	12.9	19.8	33.4	42.3	8.9
Hackney	15.9	23.2	35.7	43.5	7.8
Southwark	13.1	18.8	31.2	38.1	7.0
Haringey	11.0	18.3	30.8	37.1	6.3
Islington	13.5	17.7	31.6	37.1	5.6
Manchester	17.7	19.8	37.8	43.2	5.4
Easington	12.3	13.1	37.1	42.3	5.2
Liverpool	20.5	22.1	39.4	44.5	5.1
Glasgow City	19.9	19.7	38.5	42.9	4.5
Westminster	11.0	12.6	30.1	34.5	4.4
Lambeth	13.2	17.6	31.3	35.7	4.4
Lewisham	10.5	14.8	28.9	33.0	4.2
Greenwich	9.9	13.7	29.4	33.5	4.1
Knowsley	22.8	22.7	41.8	45.7	4.0

Note: All percentages are expressed to one decimal place.

Source: Census of Population

Table 7: Unemployment and non-employment rates for men of working age for LADs with largest increases in non-employment (1981-91) (%)

TTWA	Unemployment rate (1981)	Unemployment rate (1991)	Non-employment rate (1981)	Non-employment rate (1991)	Percentage point change in non-employment rate (1981-91)
Easington	13.7	16.9	25.3	38.3	13.0
Newham	14.6	22.6	22.4	35.0	12.6
Tower Hamlets	19.2	26.3	26.6	38.6	12.0
Hackney	18.2	26.6	27.8	39.2	11.5
Haringey	12.5	21.2	22.5	33.2	10.7
Barnsley	12.0	16.5	22.4	32.4	10.0
Cynon Valley	16.1	19.1	28.2	38.1	9.9
Wansbeck	11.0	15.5	21.8	31.6	9.8
Bolsover	8.9	13.1	19.1	28.9	9.7

Note: All percentages are expressed to one decimal place.
Source: Census of Population

Many more LADs exhibited increases in the share of men of working age non-employed: those with the largest increases are listed in Table 7. The former coalmining areas are particularly prominent within this group, with especially large increases in the proportion of older men non-employed (in Easington there was a 28 percentage point increase in the share of men aged 45-59 years non-employed between 1981 and 1991). The list of LADs in Table 7 excludes areas such as Liverpool, Knowsley and Rhondda, where at least one third of males of working age were non-employed in 1981 and where the non-employment rate in 1991 exceeded 40%.

Only those local areas with extreme values are presented in Tables 4-7. In order to provide a fuller picture of the main geographical dimensions of change at the local level, use is made of a *socioeconomic classification* of LADs (see details of the ONS classification of LADs outlined in Appendix A) in the remainder of this sub-section.

Turning first to *men of working age*, Figure 11 shows the unemployment rate, inactivity rate and non-employment rate at the time of the 1981 and 1991 Censuses, in each of six 'families' of LADs (the 'families' are ranked in descending order on percentage point change in the non-employment rate between 1981 and 1991). The following key features are evident:

- A broad 'urban–rural' distinction is apparent: with 'Inner London' and the 'mining and industrial areas' displaying the highest unemployment, inactivity and non-employment rates, and the 'rural areas' and 'prospering areas' the lowest such rates.

- Although ranked fourth out of the six 'families' on change in incidence of non-employment over the decade, the 'urban centres' display the third highest unemployment and non-employment rates.

- Although 'Inner London' witnessed the largest percentage point increase in the non-employment rate between 1981 and 1991, the 'mining and industrial areas' display higher inactivity and non-employment rates. Whereas in the former 'family' it was the marked rise in the unemployment rate which contributed to the large percentage point increase in non-employment over the period, in the latter group the increase in non-employment is a function solely of the increase in inactivity among men of working age, as the incidence of unemployment declined slightly (see Figure 12).

Figure 11: Unemployment, inactivity and non-employment rates for men of working age by LAD 'families' (1981 and 1991)

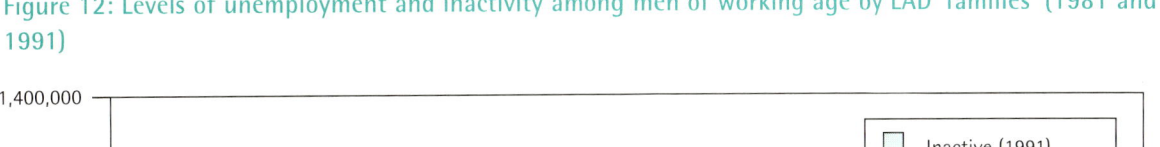

Source: Census of Population

Figure 12: Levels of unemployment and inactivity among men of working age by LAD 'families' (1981 and 1991)

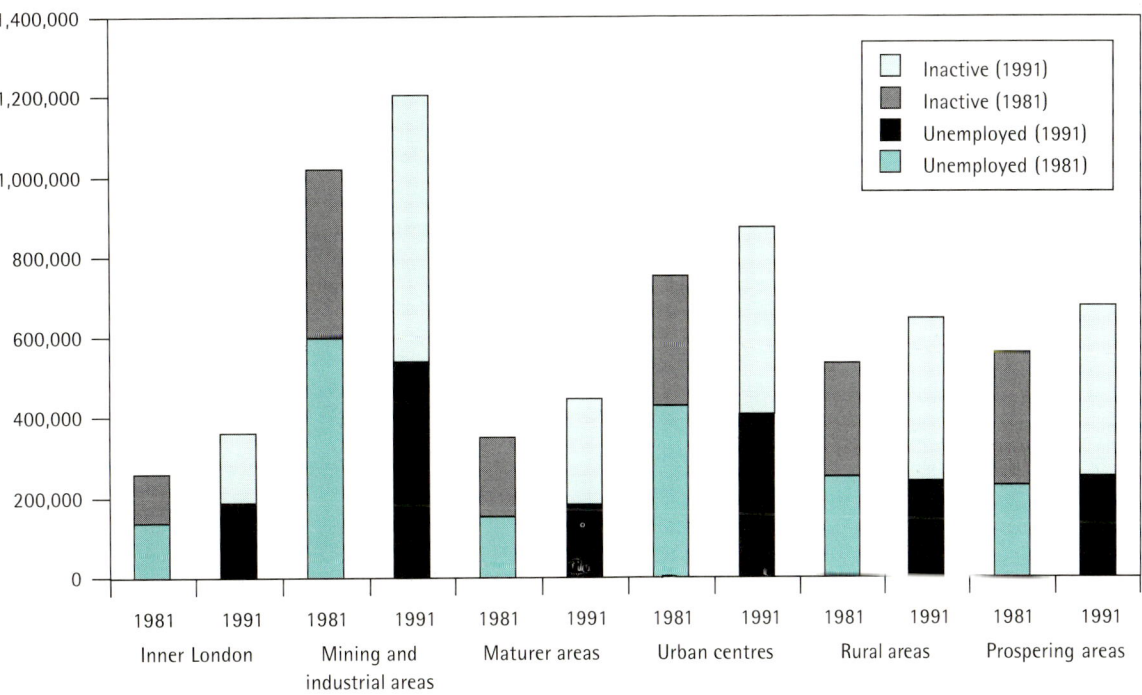

Source: Census of Population

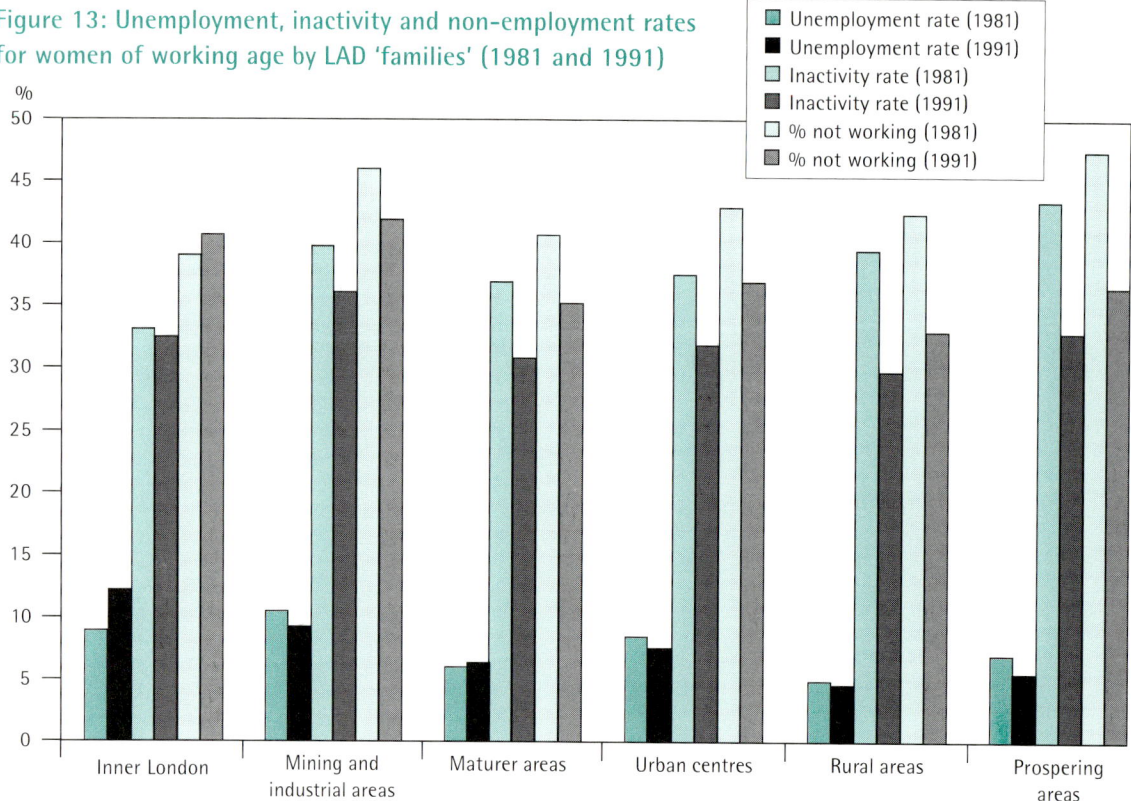

Figure 13: Unemployment, inactivity and non-employment rates for women of working age by LAD 'families' (1981 and 1991)

Legend:
- Unemployment rate (1981)
- Unemployment rate (1991)
- Inactivity rate (1981)
- Inactivity rate (1991)
- % not working (1981)
- % not working (1991)

Source: Census of Population

More detailed spatial disaggregation into 34 'clusters' further underlines the experience of increasing non-employment in larger urban areas over the decade to 1991:

- Within 'Inner London' there were increases in the non-employment rate for working age men of over 12 percentage points in 'Newham and Tower Hamlets', of nearly 9 percentage points in the 'Inner City Boroughs' and of nearly 8 percentage points in the 'Cosmopolitan Outer Boroughs'.

- The next largest increases in non-employment (about 6 percentage points) were recorded in 'areas with inner city characteristics', 'concentrations of public sector housing' and 'Glasgow and Dundee'.

- In 1991 non-employment rates for men of working age ranged from over one third in 'Newham and Tower Hamlets', 'Glasgow and Dundee', 'areas with inner city characteristics', 'concentrations of public sector housing' and 'former mining areas – Wales and Durham', to 15% or less in 'areas with transient populations' (all of these LADs contain Armed Services bases), 'growth corridors' and 'concentrations of prosperity'.

- Among men aged 45-59 years non-employment rates in 1991 ranged from 39% in the 'concentrations of public sector housing' (where the inactivity rate increased by 17

percentage points between 1981 and 1991, and the unemployment rate rose by 1 percentage point), to less than 6% in the 'concentrations of prosperity'.

For *women of working age* increase in the non-employment rate between 1981 and 1991 at the six-fold 'family' level was confined to 'Inner London' (see Figure 13) (although at the more detailed level of disaggregation to 34 'clusters' increases in the non-employment rate were recorded in 'Newham and Tower Hamlets', the 'Inner City London Boroughs', 'Central London', 'Glasgow and Dundee' and 'areas with inner city characteristics'). The 'urban–rural' distinction in fortunes was once again apparent with the 'rural areas' recording the largest decrease in non-employment (a reduction of 11 percentage points) between 1981 and 1991 (from the highest initial base), with the 'prospering areas' not far behind. Figure 14 illustrates that the reduction in female inactivity rates was by far the major contributor to the general pattern of decrease in the incidence of non-employment among women of working age over the decade.

The micro area picture

At the micro area (ward) level geographical variations in the experience of unemployment,

Figure 14: Levels of unemployment and inactivity among women of working age by LAD 'families'

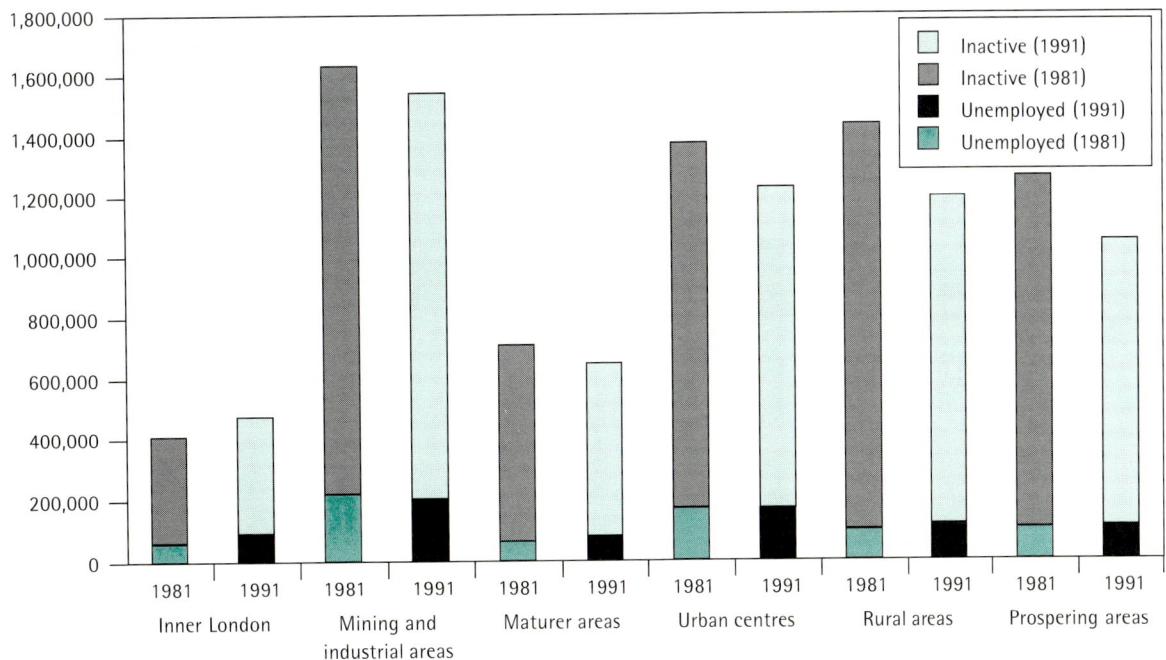

Source: Census of Population

inactivity and non-employment are even more pronounced. In order to compare the incidence of unemployment, inactivity and non-employment at the ward level, the wards were ranked into decile groups, and the median unemployment/inactivity/non-employment rate value within each decile group was calculated. Figure 15 shows the decile group median values in 1981 and 1991 for men of working age. Figures 16 and 17 present comparable data for men aged 45-59 years and women of working age, respectively.

The key features to emerge in respect of the experience of *men of working age* at the ward level (see Figure 15) are:

- Similar median values on the *unemployment rate* for all decile groups in 1981 and 1991. However, there is evidence of a very slight increase in the unemployment rate in the highest unemployment rate wards (decile group 1 in Figure 15) coupled with a slight decrease in the lowest unemployment rate wards (decile group 10 in Figure 15). This is indicative of a 'polarisation' in experience of unemployment at the micro area level over the decade.

- Higher values on the *inactivity rate* across all decile groups in 1981 compared with 1991. The percentage point increases in inactivity rates are most pronounced in the wards with the greatest incidence of inactivity among working age men.

- An increase in the *non-employment rate* for each decile group between 1981 and 1991, with increases being most pronounced in wards characterised by the highest incidence of non-employment.

For *older men* these general patterns are even more pronounced. Figure 16 shows that in the decile group with the highest values on each of the three indicators the median unemployment rate increased from 20% in 1981 to 21% in 1991, the median inactivity rate more than doubled from 14% in 1981 to 29% in 1991, and the non-employment rate rose from 29% to 41%. This highlights the *extensiveness and severity of joblessness* in the most disadvantaged wards. (At a more detailed level of spatial disaggregation [such as at the enumeration district] the geographical disparities between micro areas would be even greater.)

The picture of change is rather different for *women of working age* at the ward level (see Figure 17):

- Across all decile groups there was a reduction in the median values on the *unemployment rate*, the *inactivity rate* and the *non-employment rate*

- There is no clear evidence for a 'polarisation' in experience of unemployment, inactivity and non-employment between 1981 and 1991.

Figure 15: Unemployment, inactivity and non-employment rates for men of working age by ward

(a) Unemployment rate

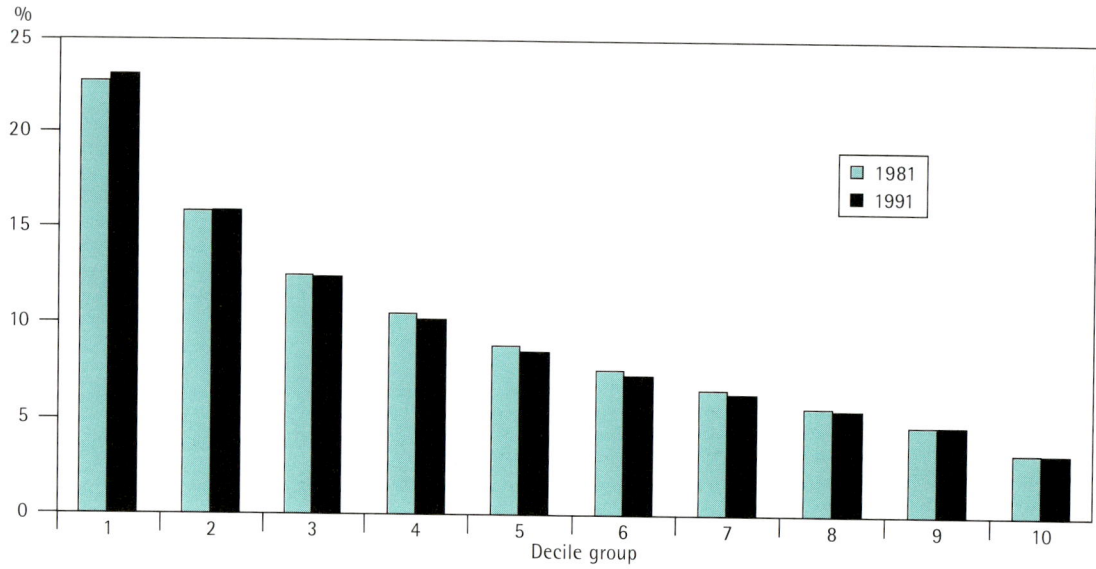

(b) Inactivity rate

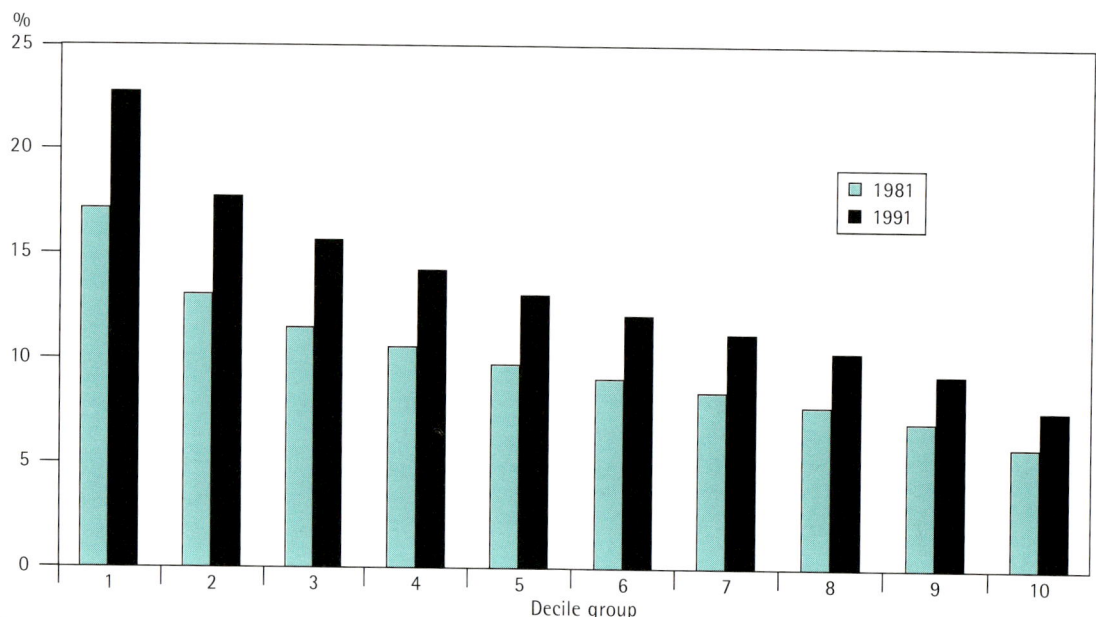

(c) Non-employment rate

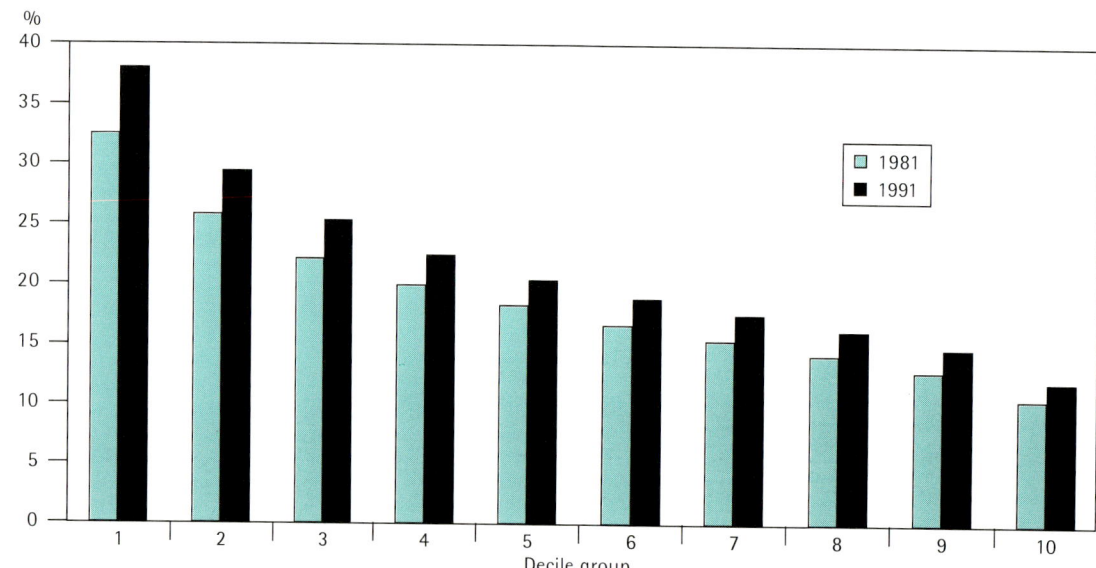

Source: Census of Population

Figure 16: Unemployment, inactivity and non-employment rates for men aged 45-59 years by ward

(a) Unemployment rate

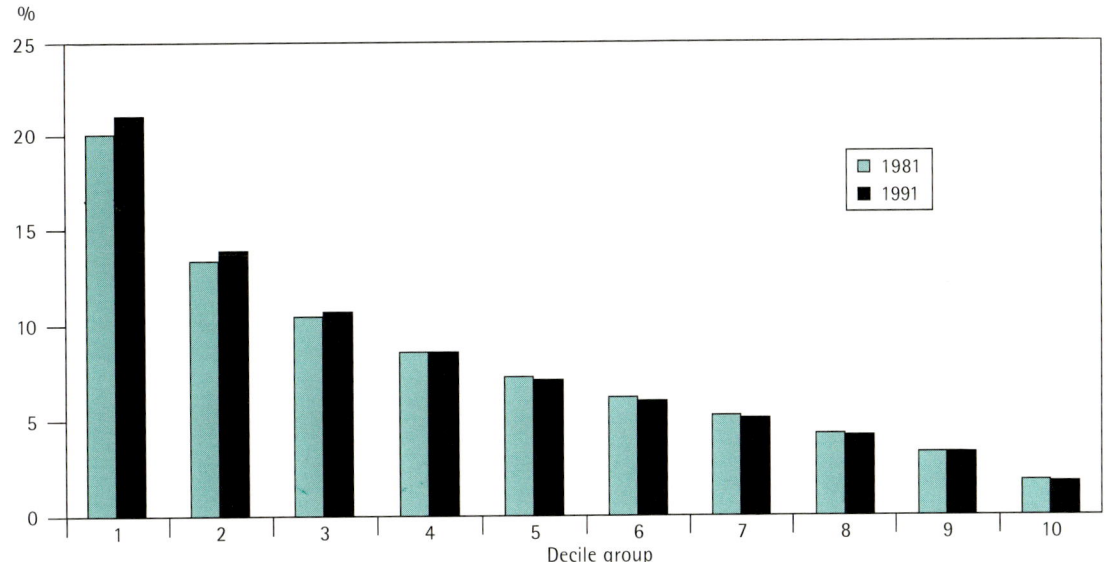

(b) Inactivity rate

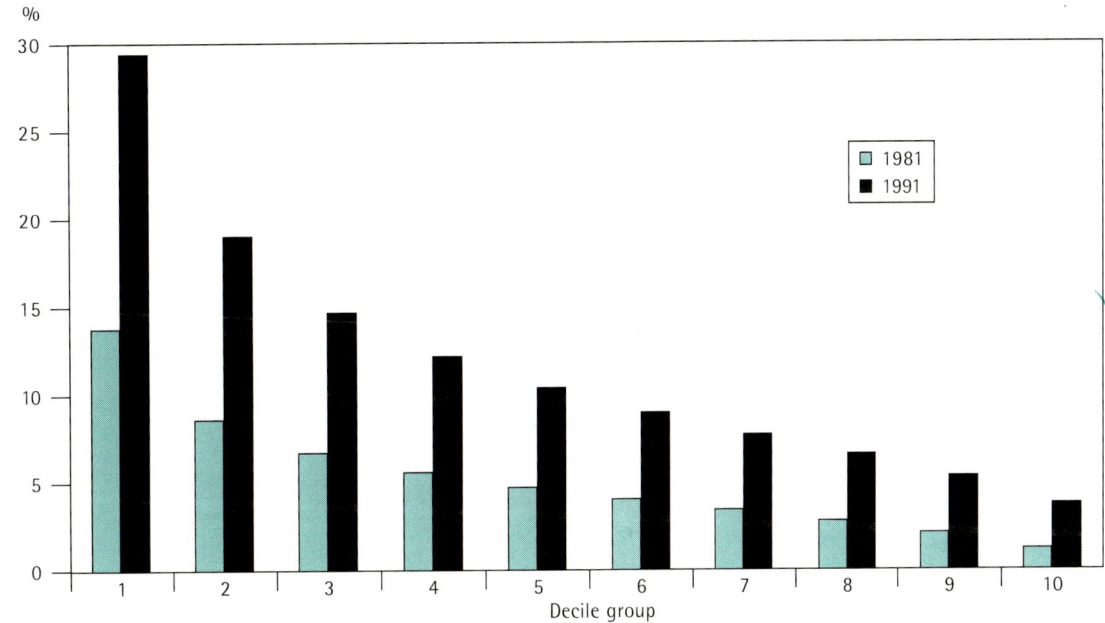

(c) Non-employment rate

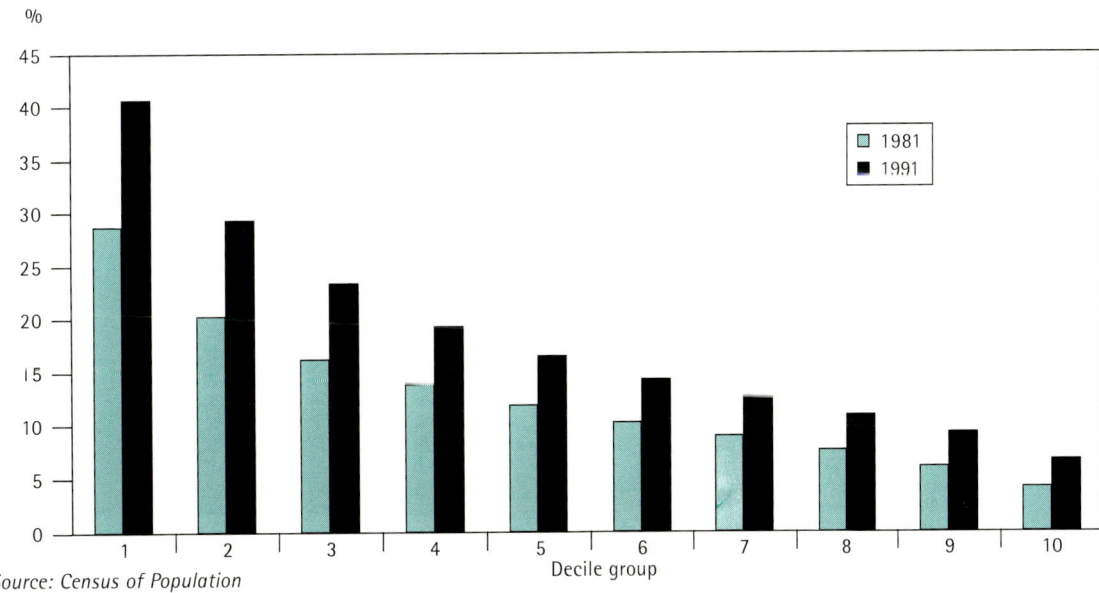

Source: Census of Population

29

Figure 17: Unemployment, inactivity and non-employment rates for women of working age by ward

(a) Unemployment rate

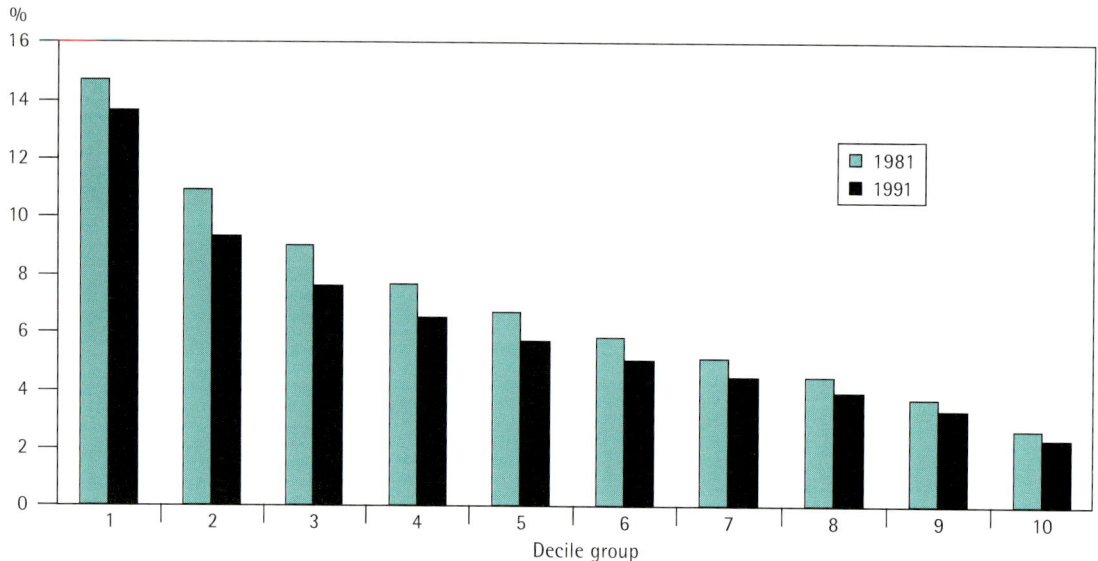

(b) Inactivity rate

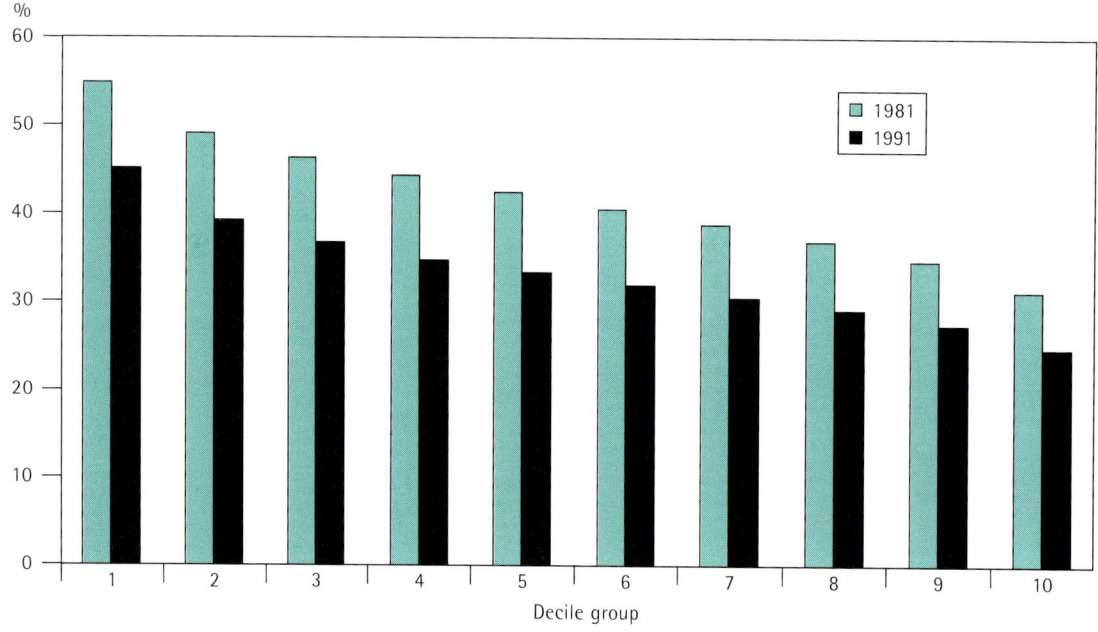

(c) Non-employment rate

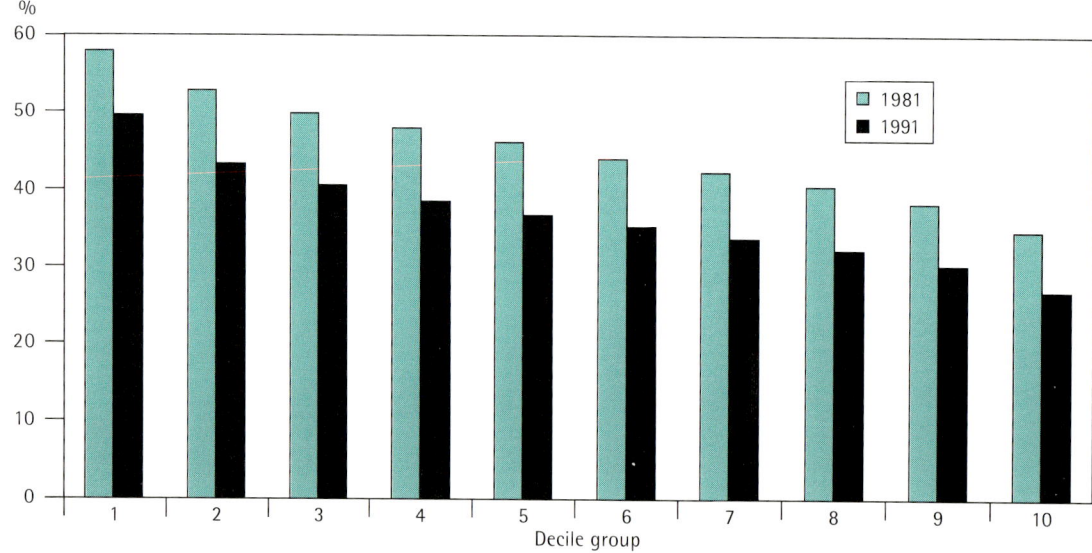

Source: Census of Population

Figures 18-20 show the incidence of male unemployment at the micro area level within Merseyside, the West Midlands Metropolitan County and Inner London in 1991.

Figure 18: The incidence of male unemployment in Merseyside (1991)

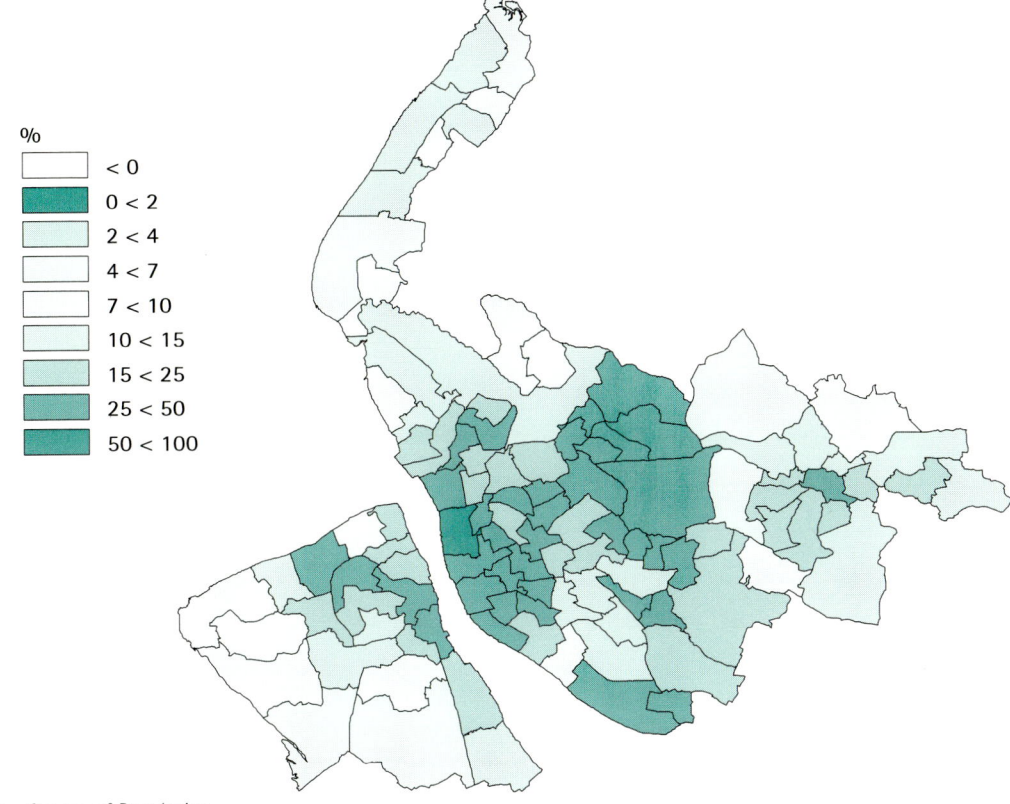

Source: Census of Population

Figure 19: The incidence of male unemployment in the West Midlands Metropolitan County (1991)

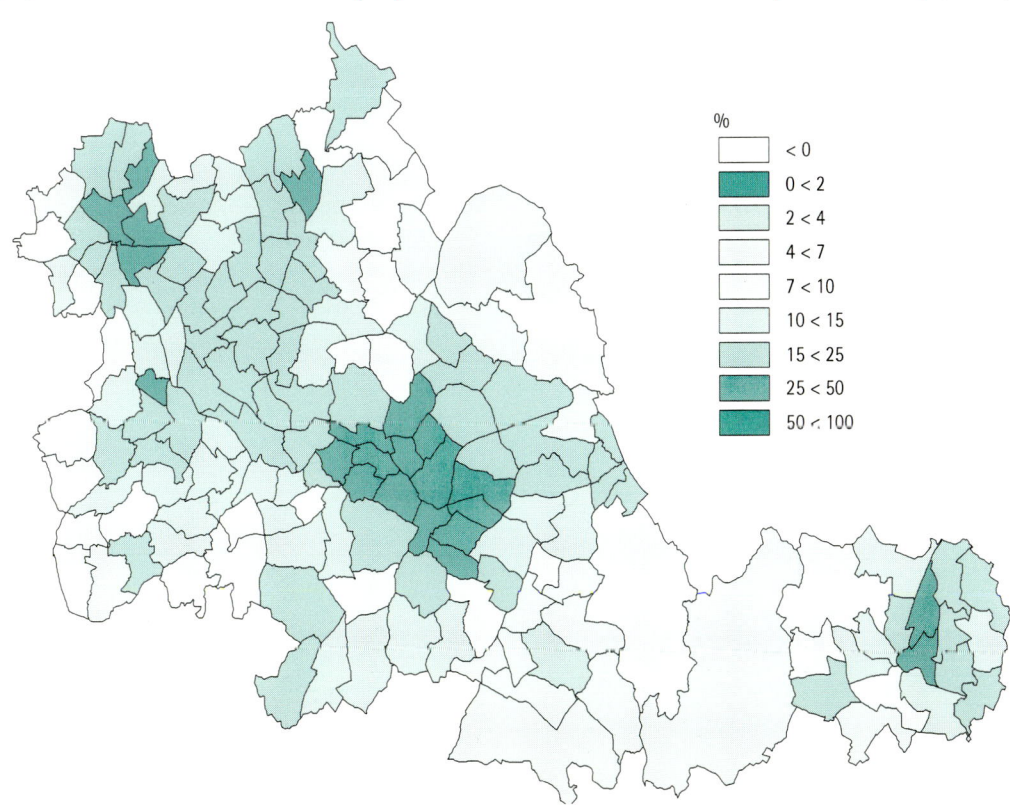

Source: Census of Population

Figure 20: The incidence of male unemployment in London (1991)

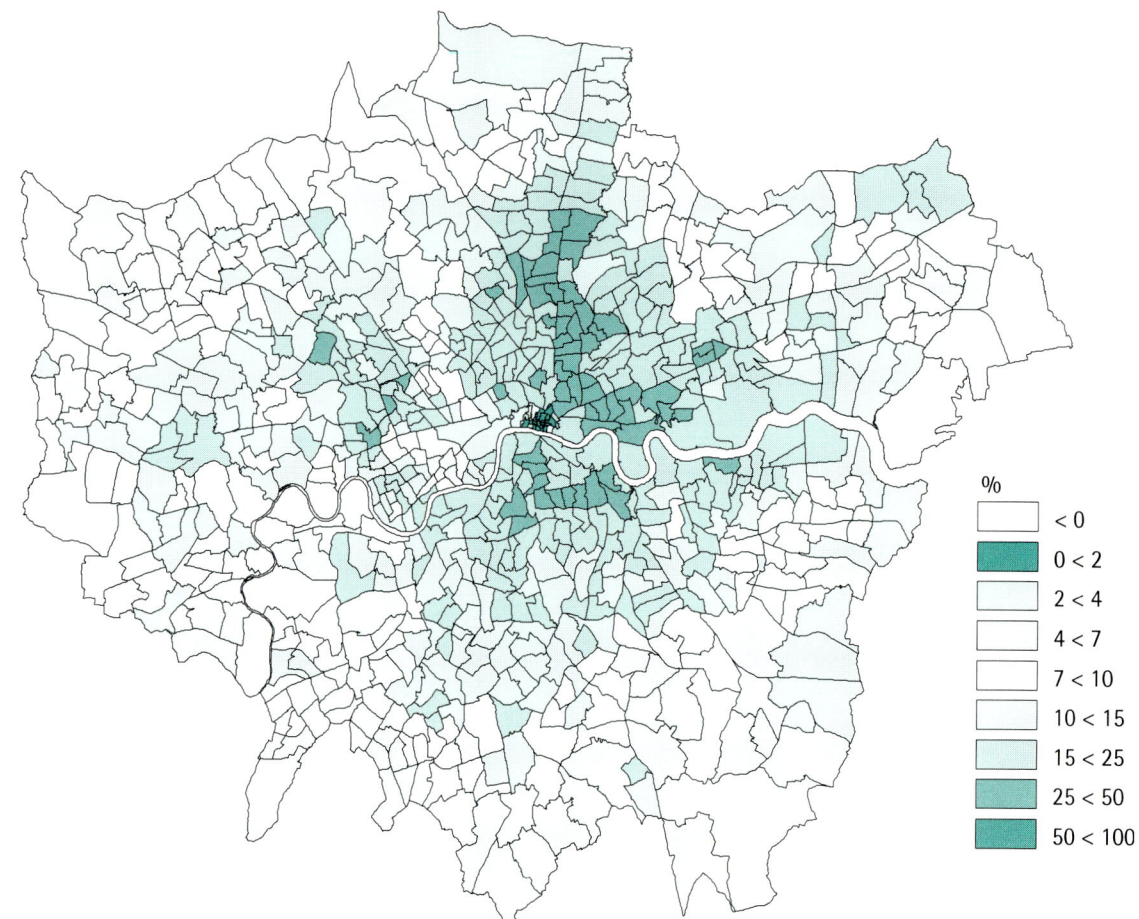

%

	< 0
	0 < 2
	2 < 4
	4 < 7
	7 < 10
	10 < 15
	15 < 25
	25 < 50
	50 < 100

Source: Census of Population

These figures highlight the existence of marked *intra-urban* variations in the incidence of male unemployment at the time of the 1991 Census of Population. In all three large urban areas there are particular concentrations of high unemployment in the inner city areas. In Figure 18 the concentrations of high unemployment in the Dockland areas of Liverpool are highlighted. In Figure 19 the wards of inner Birmingham stand out as having the highest unemployment rates and the inner city areas of Coventry (in the east) and Wolverhampton (in the west) are also highlighted. Within Greater London the largest concentrations of high unemployment are in inner London. In Merseyside, in particular (see Figure 18), the high incidence of unemployment in certain outer estates is also evident. (As noted above, these intra-urban differentials would be even more marked at the enumeration district scale.)

5

Dynamics of unemployment

Introduction

At any 'snapshot' in time the stock of unemployment (which was the focus of attention in Chapter 4) is in a constant state of flux, with newly employed people joining the stock (*on-flows*) while some other unemployed people leave the stock (*off-flows*) – for employment, inactivity, and so on. Monthly on-flows and off-flows are often extremely volatile. When, and where, on-flows exceed off-flows the stock (the level) of unemployment will rise, and vice versa. The observed unemployment stock is determined by these on-flows and off-flows and the average *duration* of unemployment. An unemployed person enters the stock, remains unemployed for some period of time and then exits the stock.

In this chapter two features of the dynamics of unemployment are analysed. First, the likelihood of becoming and ceasing to be unemployed at the local area level is examined using claimant count flow statistics, and some summary information on the duration of unemployment spells is presented (see below). Secondly, using data from the JUVOS Cohort Survey a longitudinal perspective on individual unemployment spells is provided (see p 45).

The likelihood of becoming and ceasing to be unemployed and unemployment duration

One method of standardising unemployment on-flows and off-flows is to examine the likelihood of becoming and remaining unemployed. These likelihoods are defined as follows:

- *likelihood of becoming unemployed* = on-flow over a specified time period/workforce (hence, it is possible to calculate likelihood of becoming unemployed statistics only for those areas for which workforce numbers [or estimates] are available);
- *likelihood of ceasing to be unemployed* = off-flow over a specified time period/ unemployed stock.

Different patterns of interrelationship between the likelihood of becoming unemployed and ceasing to be unemployed may be conceptualised in terms of the framework presented in Figure 21 (see also Green, 1986). Location in the various quadrants may be interpreted as follows (although it should be borne in mind that the operation of benefit regulations is likely to affect the patterns described):

- *quadrant A:* a lower than average likelihood of becoming unemployed in conjunction with a lower than average likelihood of ceasing to be unemployed – long duration unemployment is likely to be a problem in these areas;
- *quadrant B:* an unfavourable unemployment position – a higher than average likelihood of becoming unemployed and a lower than average likelihood of ceasing to be unemployed;
- *quadrant C:* a relatively favourable unemployment position – a lower than average likelihood of becoming unemployed and a greater than average likelihood of ceasing to be unemployed;
- *quadrant D:* a greater than average likelihood of becoming unemployed coupled with a higher than average likelihood of ceasing to be unemployed – this pattern is likely to be indicative of areas with seasonal/unstable employment structures.

Figure 21: Interrelationships between the likelihood of becoming unemployed and ceasing to be unemployed

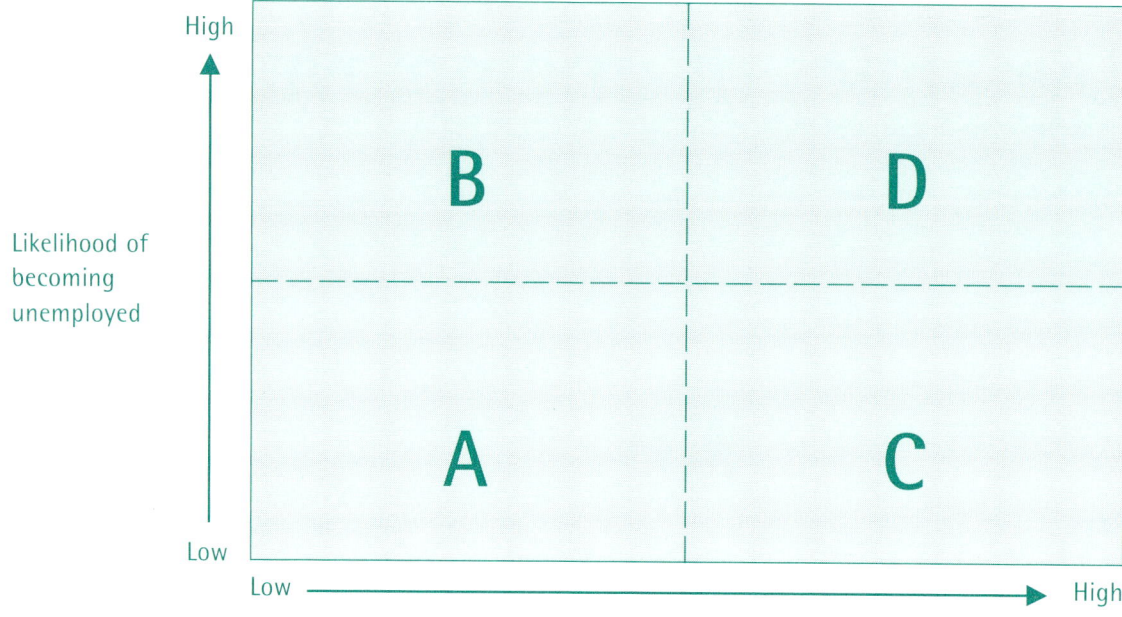

Key: — — —   National average

Table 8 shows statistics on the likelihood of becoming unemployed and the likelihood of ceasing to be unemployed for persons in three main urban areas: Merseyside, the West Midlands Metropolitan County and Inner London, compared with the national level. Information is presented for three contrasting periods:

- *Winter 1985/86:* when unemployment remained high after the massive increase in unemployment in the early 1980s;

- *Winter 1990/91:* at the end of the late 1980s boom;

- *Winter 1992/93:* around the time of the peak in unemployment in the early 1990s recession;

- *Winter 1996/97:* as unemployment continued to fall (figures in this period are likely to be affected by the onset of the Jobseeker's Allowance).

The key features emerging from an examination of figures presented in this table are:

- There is a general trend towards a reduction in the likelihood of becoming unemployed from 1986-97 across all areas. The likelihood of ceasing to be unemployed increased during the recovery periods of the late 1980s and mid-1990s, but declined slightly during the early 1990s recession.

- At each of the four 'snapshots' Merseyside is characterised by the unfavourable combination of a higher than national average likelihood of becoming unemployed coupled with a lower than average likelihood of ceasing to be unemployed (that is, location in *quadrant B* in Figure 21).

- The West Midlands Metropolitan County and Inner London are characterised by a slightly lower than national average likelihood of becoming unemployed, but a somewhat lower than average likelihood of ceasing to be unemployed (location in *quadrant A* in Figure 21) throughout most of the period. (In Winter 1996/97 there is some convergence towards the national average situation. This may reflect some 'discontinuities' associated with the introduction of the Jobseeker's Allowance.)

Table 8: Likelihood of becoming and ceasing to be unemployed in three large urban areas and Great Britain (%)

Area	Winter 1985/86	Winter 1990/91	Winter 1992/93	Winter 1996/97
Likelihood of becoming unemployed				
Merseyside	9.7	8.9	8.6	8.3
West Midlands Metropolitan County	7.6	7.4	7.4	5.7
Inner London	7.0	6.7	7.4	5.0
Great Britain	*8.2*	*7.4*	*7.9*	*5.9*
Likelihood of ceasing to be unemployed				
Merseyside	47.6	56.2	55.2	79.8
West Midlands Metropolitan County	49.3	64.0	53.7	88.9
Inner London	72.9	74.7	58.8	82.8
Great Britain	*68.6*	*83.6*	*70.2*	*83.7*

Source: *JUVOS claimant count unemployment flow statistics*

Table 9: Distribution of TTWAs by quadrant on the basis of the likelihood of becoming and ceasing to be unemployed (Winter 1992/93 and Winter 1995/96)

Quadrant	Winter 1992/93 (frequency)	Winter 1992/93 (%)	Winter 1995/96 (frequency)	Winter 1995/96 (%)
A	20	6.2	19	5.9
B	43	13.4	85	26.4
C	116	36.0	98	30.4
D	143	44.4	120	37.3

Note: *For key to quadrants see Figure 21.*

Source: *JUVOS claimant count unemployment flow statistics*

Figures 22 and 23 plot the likelihood of becoming and ceasing to be unemployed at the TTWA level in Winter 1992/93 and Winter 1995/96, while Table 9 shows the distribution of TTWAs by quadrant in each of the two time periods. TTWAs in Figures 22 and 23 are distinguished according to broad regional location ('North' and 'South') and status in the urban hierarchy ('dominant', 'subdominant' and 'freestanding'). Some of the TTWAs based on the largest cities are also distinguished.

In each of the two time periods the quadrant containing the greatest number of TTWAs is

quadrant D – characterised by a higher than average likelihood of entering and leaving unemployment. Many of the more rural areas are located in this quadrant. The second largest proportion of TTWAs is in *quadrant C* – characterised by the favourable interrelationship of a lower than average likelihood of leaving unemployment and a higher than average likelihood of leaving unemployment (Reading falls into this quadrant). In both 1992/93 and 1995/96 TTWAs from southern Britain are disproportionately located in *quadrants D* and *C*.

Figure 22: Likelihood of becoming unemployed and ceasing to be unemployed by TTWA (Winter 1992/93)

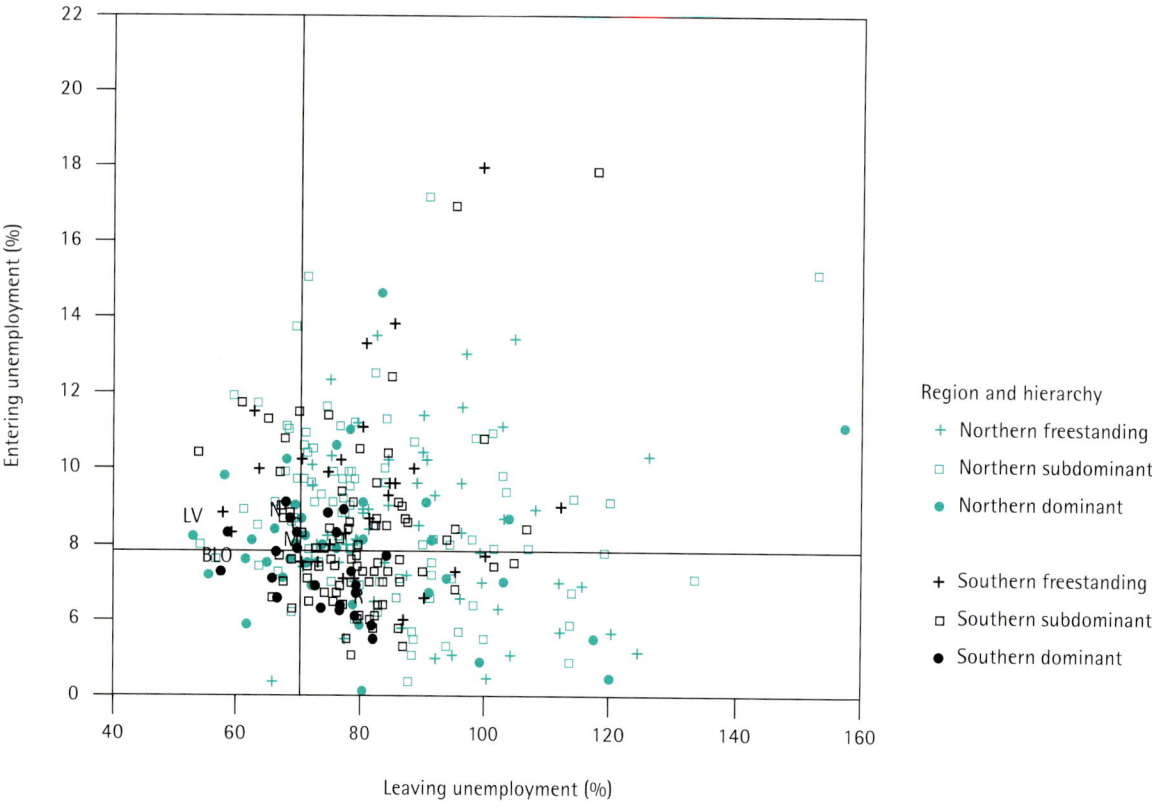

Source: JUVOS claimant count unemployment flow statistics

Figure 23: Likelihood of becoming unemployed and ceasing to be unemployed by TTWA (Winter 1995/96)

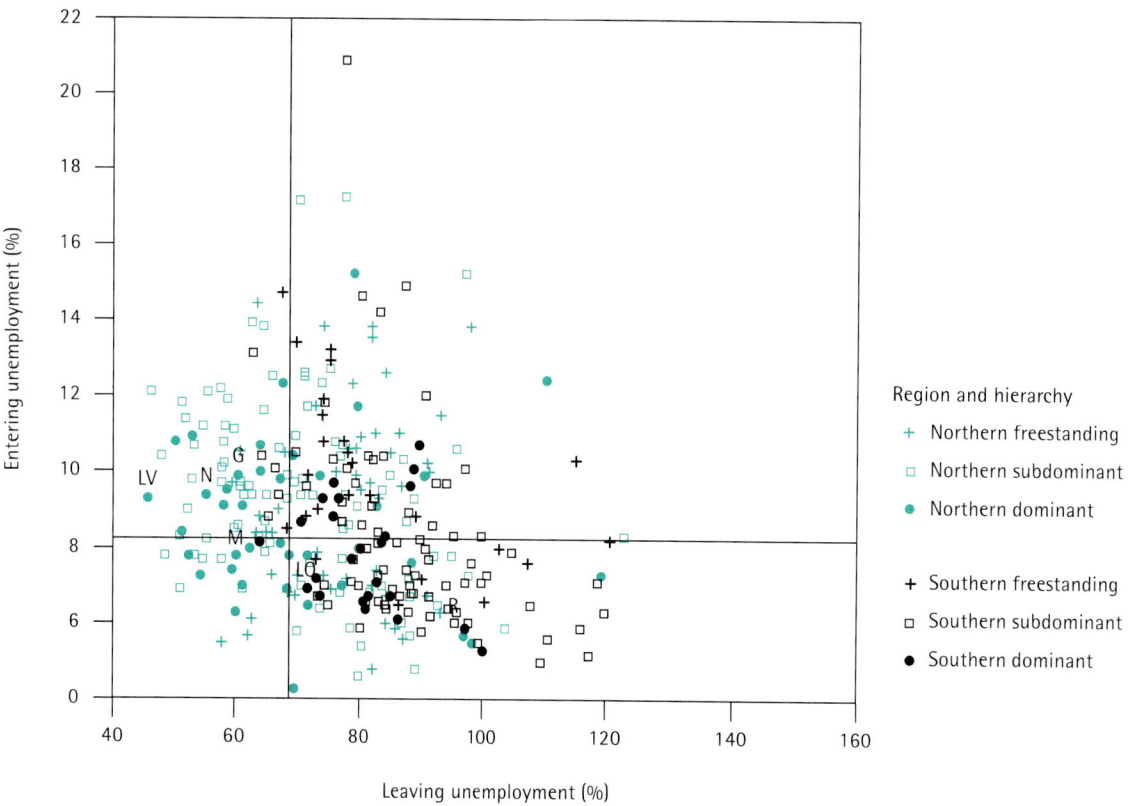

Key: B: Birmingham; G: Glasgow; LO: London; LV: Liverpool; M: Manchester; N: Newcastle; R: Reading.

Source: JUVOS claimant count unemployment flow statistics

As outlined above, those TTWAs in *quadrant B* suffer an especially unfavourable set of employment circumstances, being characterised by a higher than average likelihood of entering unemployment and a lower than average likelihood of leaving unemployment. In Winter 1992/93 13% of TTWAs fell into this category – including Liverpool, Newcastle upon Tyne and Glasgow. Many of the other largest cities fell into *quadrant A* – being characterised by a lower than average likelihood of ceasing to be unemployed and a lower than average likelihood of entering unemployment. In Winter 1995/96 26% of TTWAs were in *quadrant B*. Most of the largest cities in northern Britain were in this quadrant, with representatives from southern Britain virtually absent.

As indicated in the discussion above, areas with different interrelationships between the likelihood of becoming and ceasing to be unemployed face rather different unemployment problems. A good deal of policy emphasis is focused on *long duration unemployment*, and hence it is appropriate to consider this in more detail in the remainder of this section. Figure

24 shows the duration profile of unemployment in Great Britain from 1979-97 distinguishing:

- those unemployed for less than six months;

- those unemployed for six months or longer (the *longer-term unemployed*);

- those unemployed for 12 months or longer (the *long-term unemployed*);

- those unemployed for 24 months or longer (the *very long-term unemployed*).

As with the unemployment rate, the incidence of longer-term unemployment is higher for men than for women. Table 10 lists the 10 TTWAs with the highest incidence of long-term unemployment for men in April 1991 and April 1997, and also shows their longer-term and very long-term unemployment rates. Large urban TTWAs located in northern Britain predominate at the top of the rankings – with Liverpool, Middlesbrough, South Tyneside and Hartlepool TTWAs included in the 'top 10' in both time periods.

Table 10: TTWAs ranked on male long-term unemployment rate (April 1991 and April 1997) (%)

April 1991 TTWA	> 6 months	> 12 months	> 2 years	April 1997 TTWA	> 6 months	> 12 months	> 2 years
Cumnock and Sanquhar	8.63	7.48	5.14	Liverpool	7.32	6.41	4.67
Liverpool	8.58	7.46	5.53	Cumnock and Sanquhar	7.54	6.28	4.05
Greenock	6.82	6.05	4.58	South Tyneside	6.82	5.96	4.53
South Tyneside	7.42	6.03	3.94	Holyhead	6.55	5.80	4.05
Wick	6.44	5.54	4.12	Hartlepool	6.72	5.70	4.02
Middlesbrough	6.40	5.29	3.61	Thanet	6.46	5.61	3.88
Glasgow	5.74	4.96	3.71	Morpeth and Ashington	6.23	5.48	4.02
Girvan	5.33	4.75	3.43	Middlesbrough	6.17	5.38	3.97
Lanarkshire	5.62	4.71	3.26	Sutherland	5.87	5.25	3.50
Hartlepool	5.74	4.71	3.33	Girvan	5.80	5.15	3.77

Source: JUVOS claimant count unemployment duration statistics

Figure 24: The duration profile of unemployment, Great Britain (1979-97)
(a) Males

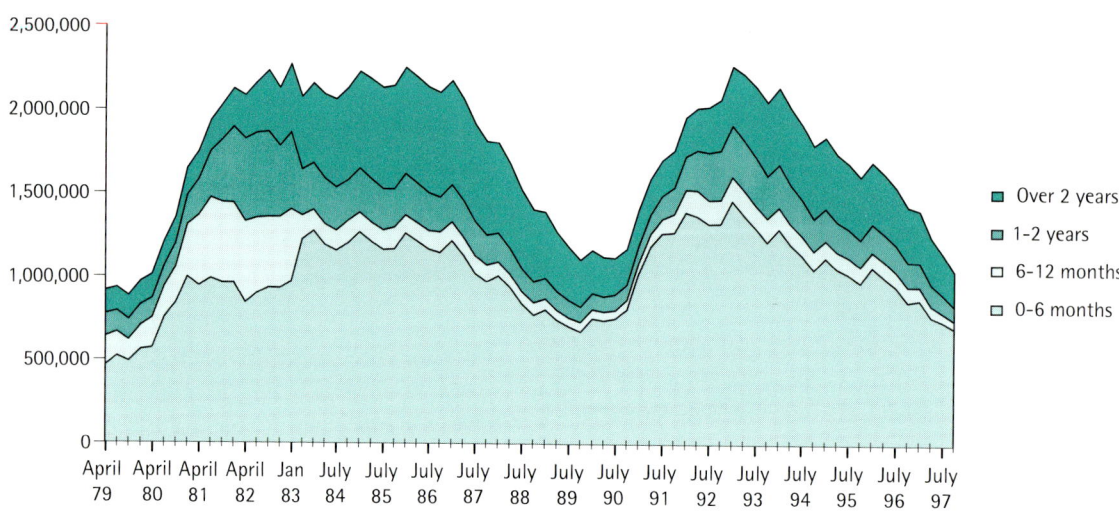

(b) Females

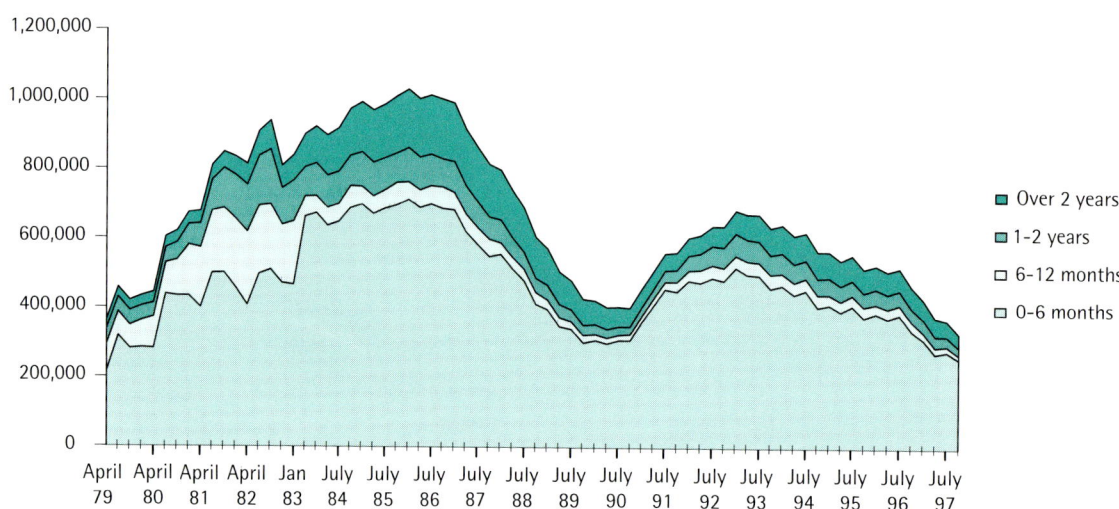

(c) Persons

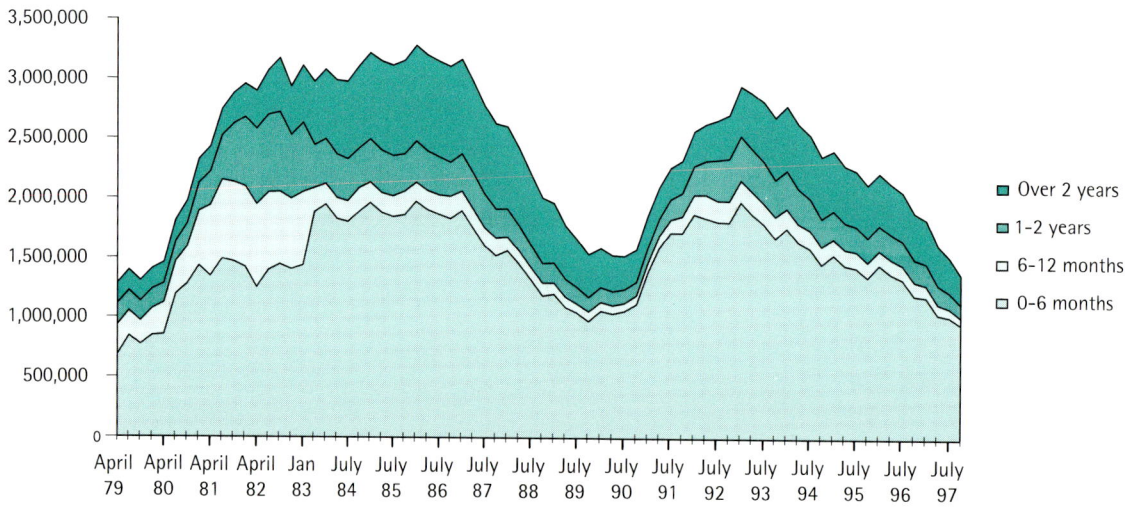

Source: JUVOS claimant count unemployment duration statistics

Figure 25: The incidence of longer-term unemployment by TTWA class (1991)

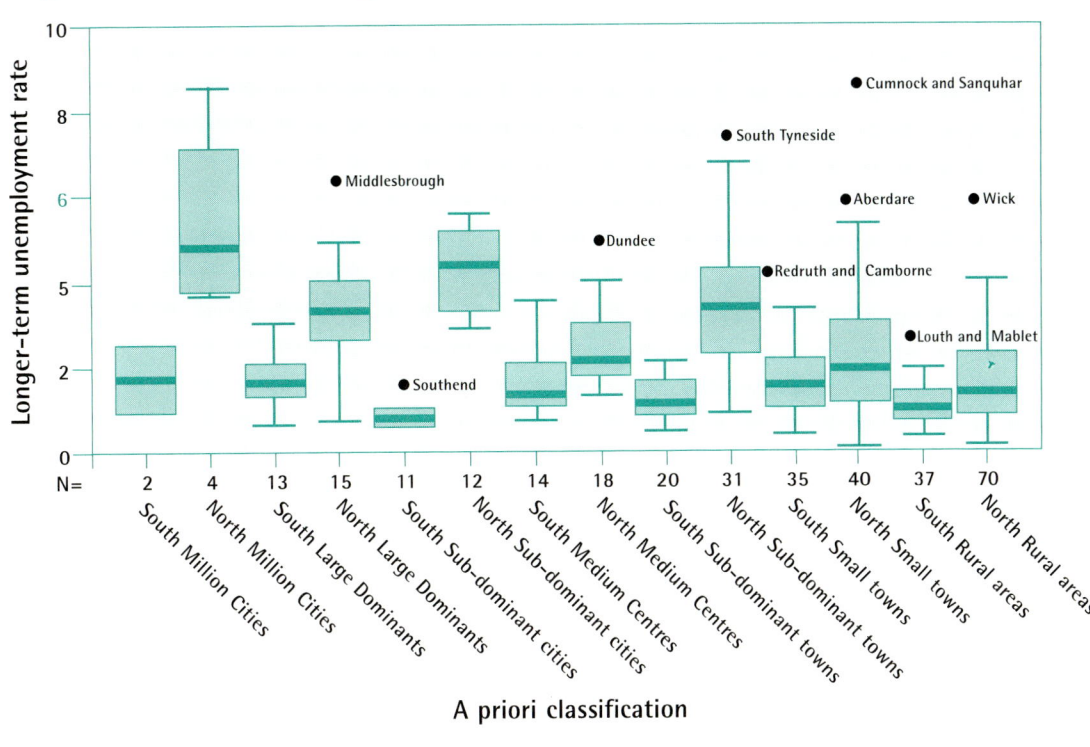

Source: JUVOS claimant count unemployment duration statistics

Figure 26: The incidence of longer-term unemployment by TTWA class (1997)

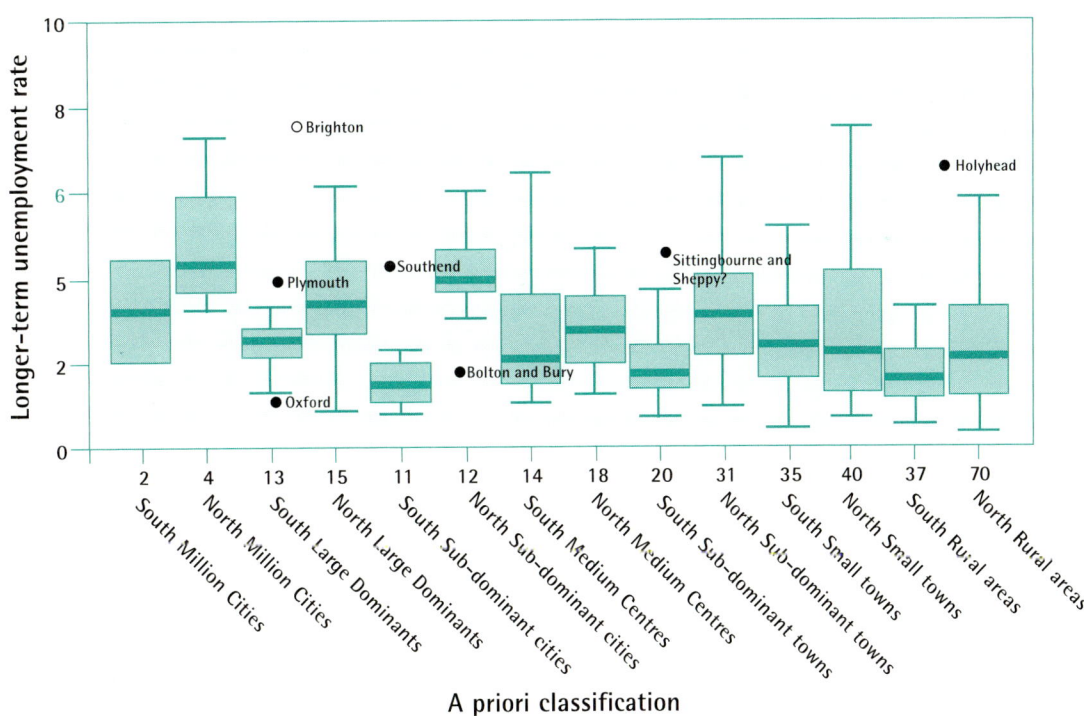

Source: JUVOS claimant count unemployment duration statistics

A fuller picture of the extent of spatial variation in the incidence of longer-term unemployment (unemployed for at least six months) at the TTWA level is provided by Figures 25 and 26, which shows the variation within and between TTWA classes in April 1991 and 1997. (These diagrams are 'box-and-whisker' plots, showing the distribution of data values for each category depicted, based on Tukey exploratory data analysis principles. The box represents the area covered by the middle 50% of the distribution [from the lower quartile to the upper quartile]. The thick horizontal line marks the median. The 'whiskers' are drawn out to the upper and lower extremes of the distribution, and TTWAs with extreme values [defined as 'outliers'] are labelled.) At both time dates a clear regional distinction is evident, with a higher incidence of longer-term unemployment in northern than in southern Britain at most levels of the urban hierarchy. Longer-term unemployment rates are highest in the metropolitan cities of northern Britain.

At the *intra-urban* level there are marked variations in the incidence of severe unemployment. Figures 27-29 show the distribution of long-term unemployed men (those unemployed for at least 12 months) as a percentage of economically active men at the micro area level in Merseyside, the West Midlands Metropolitan County and London in 1991.

Figure 27: The incidence of male long-term unemployment in Merseyside (1991)

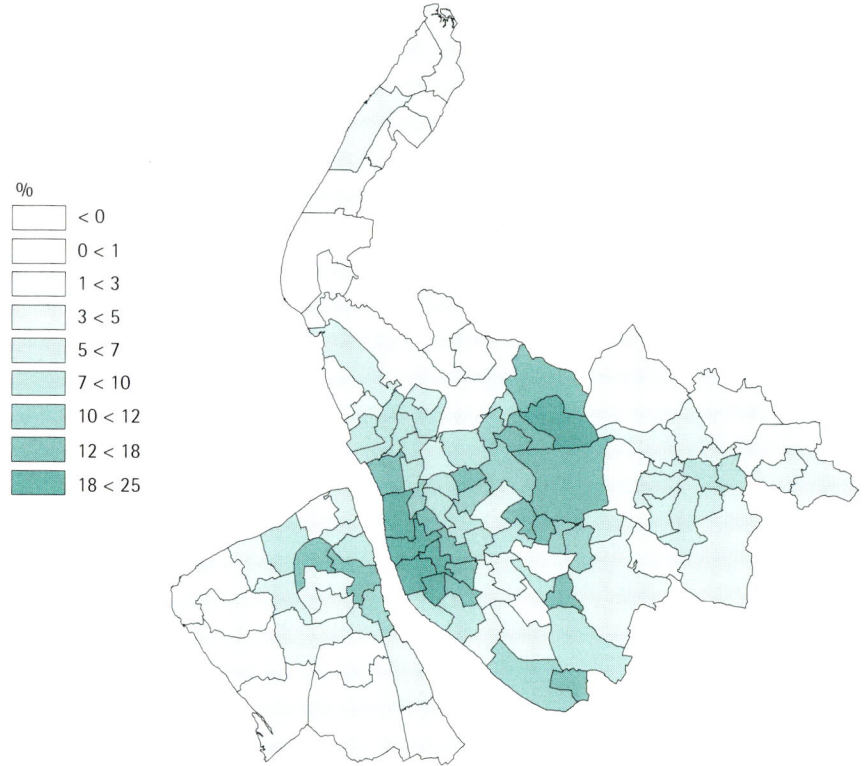

Source: JUVOS claimant count unemployment duration statistics; 1991 Census of Population

Figure 28: The incidence of male long-term unemployment in the West Midlands Metropolitan County (1991)

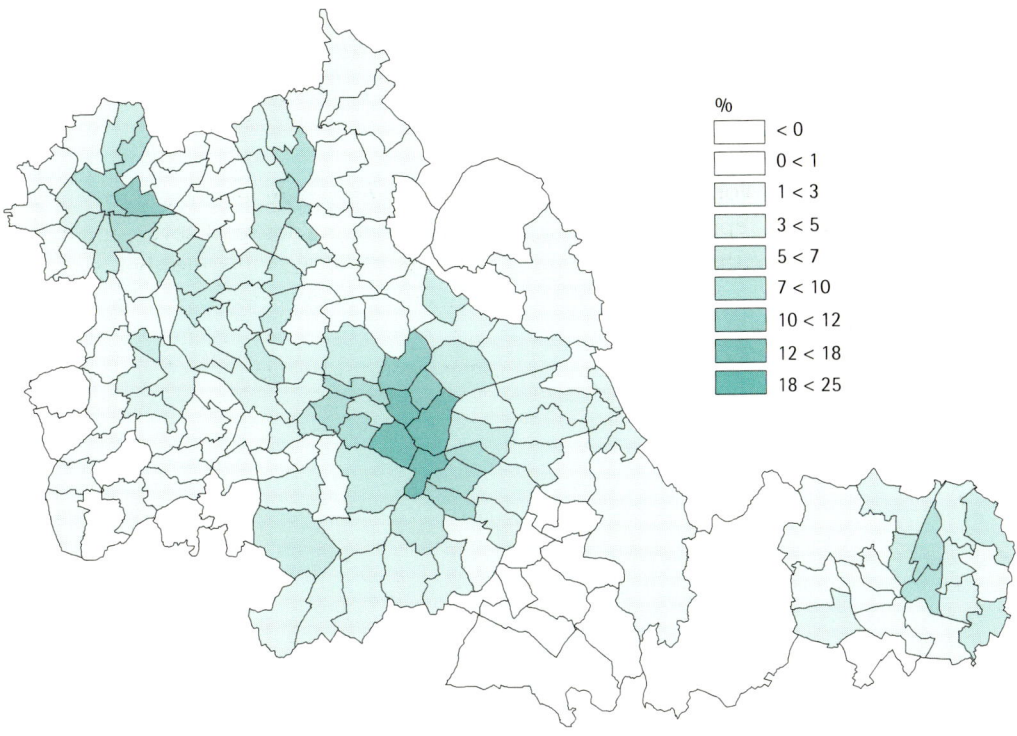

Source: JUVOS claimant count unemployment duration statistics; 1991 Census of Population

Figure 29: The incidence of male long-term unemployment in London (1991)

Source: JUVOS claimant count unemployment duration statistics; 1991 Census of Population

Table 11: Median duration of completed unemployment spells by LAD 'families' (weeks)

LAD 'family'	1986	1990	1993	1996
25%				
Rural areas	3.8	3.1	4.7	4.3
Prospering areas	3.3	2.8	5.0	4.3
Maturer areas	3.4	3.0	5.2	5.0
Urban centres	3.9	3.4	5.4	5.0
Mining and industrial areas	4.4	3.8	5.1	4.9
Inner London	3.8	3.9	6.6	7.3
50%				
Rural areas	12.1	8.4	13.4	12.5
Prospering areas	10.2	7.2	14.0	12.4
Maturer areas	10.9	8.4	15.6	15.6
Urban centres	13.0	9.8	16.6	15.1
Mining and industrial areas	15.2	11.6	15.6	15.2
Inner London	12.5	12.1	20.2	23.2
75%				
Rural areas	33.0	23.0	33.8	32.8
Prospering areas	29.6	20.2	35.3	33.3
Maturer areas	30.9	23.5	37.6	38.8
Urban centres	37.6	27.1	39.8	38.1
Mining and industrial areas	41.4	32.8	38.6	38.9
Inner London	36.8	33.4	47.8	57.7

Source: JUVOS claimant count unemployment flow statistics

As was the case for the unemployment rate (see Chapter 4) the most marked concentrations of long-term unemployment are in the inner urban areas. However, these maps also highlight the much more persistent nature of unemployment in inner and outer city Liverpool and Birkenhead, compared with London and the West Midlands conurbation.

Further insights into variations in the duration of unemployment may be gained by examining the *duration profiles* of completed unemployment spells. Table 11 presents information on the lower quartile, median and upper quartile values (in weeks) from such frequency distributions of completed unemployment spells by LAD 'family' at four points in time: 1986, 1990, 1993 and 1996.

The key features emerging are:

- In 1986 the average duration of completed unemployment spells tended to be longer in 'mining and industrial areas' than in other LAD 'families'. The 'urban centres' and 'Inner London' were also characterised by longer duration unemployment spells than the 'prospering areas', 'maturer areas' and 'rural areas'.

- By 1990 completed unemployment spells in 'Inner London' were of a similar average duration to those in the 'mining and industrial areas'. The 'prospering areas' were characterised by the shortest completed unemployment spells of any LAD 'family'.

- In 1993 and 1996 the average duration of completed unemployment spells tended to be shortest in the 'rural areas' and the 'prospering areas', while the longest duration unemployment spells occurred in 'Inner London'. The statistics presented in Table 11 further underline the deteriorating unemployment situation in 'Inner London' relative to the rest of Great Britain. In previous years the duration profiles of completed unemployment spells in 'mining and industrial areas' and 'urban centres' had not been dissimilar to the profile for 'Inner London'. The evidence presented here, alongside that in Chapter 4, suggests that a greater share of the longer duration unemployment spells were translated into inactivity in the two former LAD 'families' than in 'Inner London'.

Figure 30: Frequency distribution of unemployment spells (1982–97)

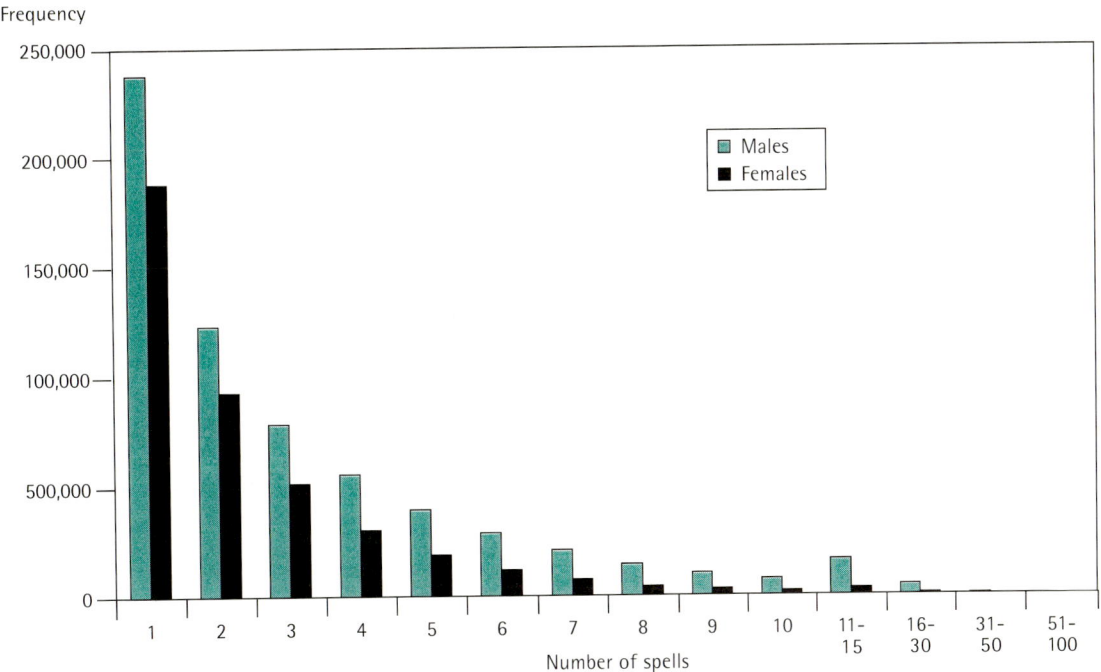

Source: JUVOS Cohort Survey

Longitudinal perspectives on unemployment

Although an analysis of unemployment flow data (as in p 35) can provide some insights into the dynamics of unemployment, to gain a more complete picture of the impact and experience of unemployment at the individual level it is necessary to link unemployment spells in individual work histories. In order to gain a longitudinal perspective on spells of unemployment within individual work histories some preliminary analyses for this study were undertaken using the JUVOS Cohort Survey. This is a longitudinal database of 5% of all claims (selected by reference to the individual's National Insurance number) for unemployment-related benefits covering the period from October 1982 to 1997. From 1995 and 1996 information on the individual's occupation and destination, respectively, are available. For the purposes of geographical analyses Cohort members were allocated to Standard Regions and LLMAs (on the basis of the Unemployment Benefit Office and postcode district codes).

Figure 30 shows the frequency distribution of unemployment spells for all individuals included in the Cohort over the entire period 1982-97. (To have an 'observation' in the Cohort an individual has to have had at least one unemployment spell.) Two out of five individuals in the Cohort had only one unemployment spell during the period, one in five had two spells and one in eight had three spells. One in four individuals recorded four or more spells of receipt of unemployment-related benefits, and one in 20 of the total had 10 or more spells. The 'shape' of the frequency distributions for number of spells are similar for men and women, although overall males account for a larger share of all unemployment spells.

Figure 31 shows the mean number of unemployment spells by age. The average man in the Cohort has experienced 3.2 unemployment spells, while the average woman has experienced 2.4 unemployment spells. Aside from those in the oldest age group identified, those aged between 20 and 34 have the largest mean number of unemployment spells. (The oldest members of the 20-34-year-old age group would have faced a labour market characterised by mass unemployment throughout their working lives [unlike older people].)

43

Figure 31: Mean number of unemployment spells by age and gender (1982–97)

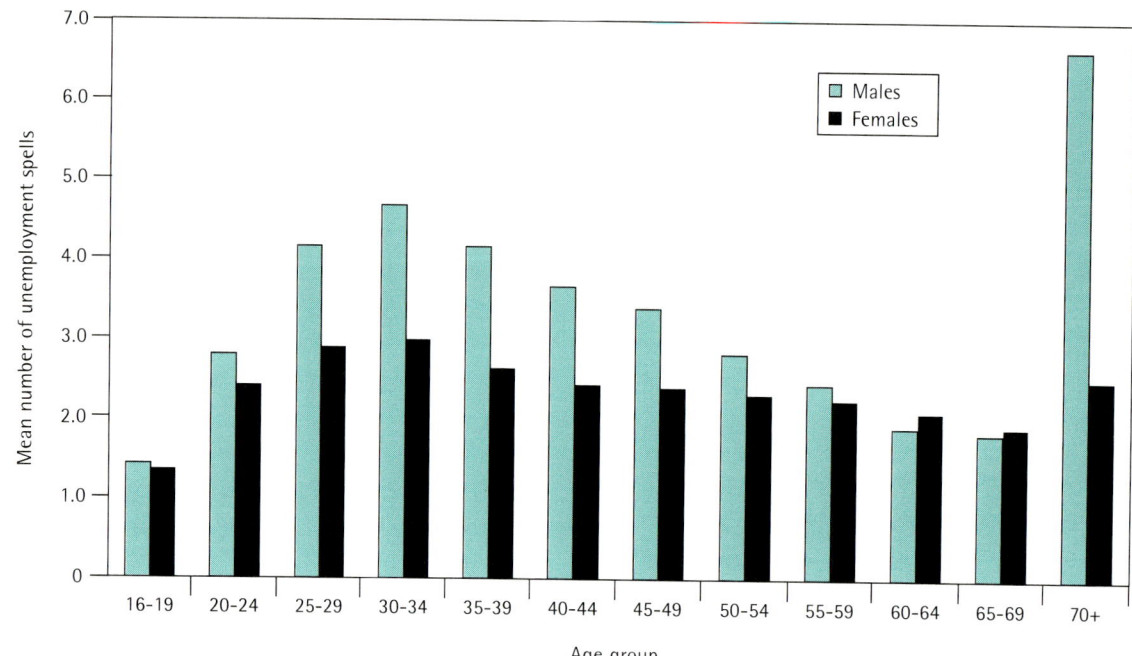

Source: JUVOS Cohort Survey

Analyses by alternative geographical frameworks (the analyses are based on location at the time of the last unemployment spell) reveal no marked spatial variations in the average number of unemployment spells recorded by Cohort members. In particular, there is no marked urban–rural differential, although individuals in Merseyside and Inner London display a higher mean number of unemployment spells than the national average. Moreover, at the regional level men in the Northern region, Wales and Scotland tend to suffer slightly more unemployment spells than those in other regions.

The scope for analyses of the *destinations* of those leaving unemployment is restricted due to the relatively large number of Cohort members (approximately one third of the total) for whom the destination is unknown. However, a number of important features are evident from an initial analysis:

- The proportion moving from unemployment into work declines with age (underlining the higher inactivity rates among those individuals in the older age groups outlined in Chapter 4).

- Those unemployed with a 'usual' or 'sought' occupation in the professional occupations

group are most likely to have 'found work', while those in other (unskilled) occupations are least likely to have 'found work'.

- An 'urban–rural' differential is evident in the proportion of those unemployed 'finding work', with those in the largest urban areas least likely to have 'found work' as their destination, followed by those in cities, while those in rural areas are the most likely to have 'found work'.

- Cohort members in the Northern region, the North West, Wales, Scotland, Yorkshire and Humberside and the West Midlands are more likely than average to move from unemployment to claim sickness or another benefit.

Information relating to the *duration* of unemployment spells from the JUVOS Cohort Survey underlines some of the key features outlined above:

- The *labour market disadvantage of those in other (unskilled) occupations:* those in other (unskilled) occupations tend to have longer than average unemployment spells overall, and are likely to experience a longer than average duration of unemployment before moving into work.

- The *labour market disadvantage of those in the largest urban areas:* those in the largest urban areas tend to have longer than average unemployment spells overall, and are likely to experience a longer than average duration of unemployment before moving into work.

The labour market circumstances facing those in other (unskilled) occupations are examined in more detail in Chapter 6.

6

Match and mismatch

Introduction

Two main paradigms may be identified in policy debates about the causes of urban unemployment/joblessness (Kasarda and Kwok-fai Ting, 1996):

- a *structural, non-voluntaristic perspective:* which emphasises the roles of urban economic change, residential segregation, and *skills and spatial mismatches* in 'explaining' unemployment/joblessness (see Holzer, 1991; Kain, 1968; 1992; Wilson, 1987);

- a *rational choice, voluntaristic perspective:* which contends that the generosity and ready availability of welfare programmes have removed the incentive for poor persons to accept low-paying jobs is the primary factor in 'explaining' unemployment/joblessness (see Mead, 1989; Murray, 1984).

In this chapter the emphasis is on exploring the role of *mismatches* by presenting empirical evidence on changing job profiles and the characteristics of the unemployed.

In examining *mismatch* it is useful to make a distinction between:

- *Skills mismatch:* this 'explanation' of unemployment focuses specifically on '*who they are*' by considering the changes in the (im)balance between the characteristics of the jobs and the potential workers available to do those jobs. In the North American literature particular emphasis is placed on the transformation of the structure of urban economies from centres of goods-processing to centres of information exchange.

Although jobs exist and are 'spatially' accessible, they are *not* 'functionally' accessible to less skilled/less well educated residents.

- *Spatial mismatch:* this 'explanation' of unemployment focuses specifically on '*where they are*' by considering demand-side factors and the geographical mismatch between residences of the unemployed and potential workplaces (Webster, 1997). According to this hypothesis high concentrations of unemployment and long-term unemployment are due to the loss of manual jobs from particular local areas with large manual workforces. A classic example of such spatial mismatch is the estate of Penrhys in the Rhondda, South Wales, where unemployment rocketed after the run down of coalmining:

There's ninety-five per cent unemployment on the site. When the pits were open it was the other way around, ninety-five per cent were employed. (Danziger, 1996, p 315)

In reality, however, skills mismatches may be compounded by spatial mismatches, as the localised loss of low-skilled jobs leads to greater spatial and skills mismatches for large numbers of urban residents with limited education. In objective terms not only may the 'opportunity structure' facing less skilled residents in areas of employment loss be relatively disadvantageous when compared with that facing more skilled residents in areas of employment growth, but there may also be subjective spatial variations in perceived opportunity sets which may compound the objective disadvantage (Galster and Killen, 1995). Moreover, segregation tendencies in urban housing markets (Haughton et al, 1993; Lee, 1994) are, in turn, likely to exacerbate such differences, and hence problems of mismatch.

Changing job profiles at the local level

The main sources of information on changing job profiles at the local level are the Annual Employment Survey (which has replaced the Census of Employment) and the Census of Population. The Labour Force Survey also contains information on employment structures disaggregated to the regional and county levels. Use is made of all of these sources in the remainder of this section.

The travel-to-work area picture

First, considering workplace-based employment change at the TTWA level, Table 12 lists those

TTWAs with the largest relative losses in employment over the decade from 1981 to 1991 (for technical details of the Census of Population Special Workplace Statistics on which these figures are based see Appendix B; it is important to note that the analyses based on Special Workplace Statistics data are restricted to England and Wales, because such data for Scotland in 1981 were not available to the authors). The loss in male full-time jobs was even more marked than the total employment loss. The decrease in the proportion of employment in manufacturing is indicative of changes in the industrial structure of employment, while the increase in the proportion of employment in managerial and professional occupations highlights the shift in the occupational structure of employment in favour of high level manual occupations. The increase in the proportion of employment in managerial and professional occupations is particularly marked in the large urban areas.

Table 12: Change in employment by TTWA (1981-91)

TTWA	% total change	% male full-time change	% employment in manufacturing		% managerial/ professional employment	
	1981-91	1981-91	1981	1991	1981	1991
South Tyneside	-11.9	-28.9	32.1	20.8	19.8	26.9
Liverpool	-10.5	-21.0	27.1	17.4	24.6	31.4
Aberdare	-9.3	-21.1	31.7	30.1	19.9	24.6
Neath and Port Talbot	-7.8	-19.3	37.9	32.9	18.6	24.9
Hartlepool	-7.5	-19.9	36.2	26.8	21.1	27.5
Mansfield	-5.8	-23.0	19.8	16.0	17.0	24.0
Burnley	-5.6	-18.4	46.9	35.2	23.0	29.1
Sheffield	-3.5	-15.9	36.6	24.0	23.9	30.9
Barnsley	-2.9	-15.6	24.1	23.5	19.3	25.0
Morpeth & Ashington	-2.5	-22.5	19.8	18.2	20.0	30.2

Source: Census of Population, Special Workplace Statistics – Set B, 1981 and 1991

The local authority district picture

Tables 13 and 14 present similar information on the changing structure of employment by LAD 'family'. In Table 13 the 'families' are ranked in ascending order on percentage employment change over the decade from 1981. 'Inner London' suffered the largest employment losses, while the 'urban centres' and 'mining and industrial areas' recorded the smallest gains. The largest relative increase in employment occurred in the 'rural areas'. (Once again, LADs in Scotland are excluded from these analyses.) Information is also presented on the change in male full-time employment and in female full-time and part-time employment. Similar geographical patterns are evident for disaggregated employment change. More detailed spatial disaggregations of LADs into 'groups' and 'clusters' reveals that after 'Inner London' the largest employment losses occurred in the 'manufacturing' and 'coalfields' 'groups', and in the 'areas with inner city characteristics' 'cluster'.

The statistics presented in Table 14 highlight two key dimensions of the changing structure of employment by 'family'. The distinctiveness of the 'Inner London' family, with a very low share of employment in manufacturing and a very high proportion in managerial and professional occupations is apparent. By contrast, the 'urban centres' and 'mining and industrial areas' have the largest proportions of employment in manufacturing (although these proportions declined over the decade), and the smallest shares in managerial and professional occupations. The shift in the industrial structure of employment from manufacturing to services and in the occupational structure from low skill to managerial and professional occupations is apparent in all areas.

Table 13: Change in employment by LAD 'family' (1981–91)

LAD 'family'	% total employment change	% male full-time employment change	% female full-time employment change	% female part-time employment change
Inner London	-3.5	-14.0	0.8	-3.8
Urban centres	16.1	3.0	16.6	32.7
Mining and industrial areas	24.1	8.6	26.9	39.7
Prospering areas	29.0	16.5	24.0	47.4
Maturer areas	35.4	22.5	32.5	42.5
Rural areas	40.7	23.5	36.0	68.4

Source: Census of Population, Special Workplace Statistics – Set B, 1981 and 1991

Table 14: Change in structure of employment by LAD 'family' (1981–91)

LAD 'family'	% employment in manufacturing		% employment in managerial/ professional occupations	
	1981	1991	1981	1991
Inner London	16.6	9.8	34.7	45.4
Urban centres	36.7	25.7	25.0	31.2
Mining and industrial areas	31.2	23.5	23.4	29.7
Prospering areas	30.6	21.1	28.6	34.2
Maturer areas	21.3	13.6	30.5	36.4
Rural areas	26.3	20.5	27.5	30.1

Source: Census of Population, Special Workplace Statistics – Set B, 1981 and 1991

Recent and projected employment change in three large urban areas

As well as examining local employment change over historical periods, it is also useful to look forwards to assess likely employment trends over the short and medium terms. In this study this has been achieved through utilising projections prepared using the Local Economy Forecasting Model (this software was developed by the Institute for Employment Research, University of Warwick, in collaboration with Cambridge Econometrics). Utilising data from a range of sources (including the Labour Force Survey, the Census of Population and the Census of Employment/Annual Employment Survey), the projections show what the economy of a local area *might* look like in the future, based on the assumption that past trends and patterns of behaviour will continue. Employment projections were generated for the three large urban areas considered in Chapters 4 and 5: Merseyside, the West Midlands conurbation, and Inner London.

To provide an overview of the *changing industrial structure* of employment in these three large urban areas, Table 15 identifies those industries in which employment is projected to decline by 10% or more over the period from 1994-2005, and those in which employment is projected to grow by 10% or more (it should be noted that some of the increases are from a relatively small initial base). Those industries projected to witness a decline or growth in employment of at least 10% in each of the three urban areas are highlighted. Key features emerging are:

- all of those industries highlighted as 'losers' across all three areas are from the primary, manufacturing and utilities sectors;

- those industries projected to record employment growth of at least 10% in each of the three areas – notably, professional services, computing services and other business services – are representatives of the service sector;

- in Inner London employment is projected to decline by 10% or more in the majority of primary and manufacturing industries.

Table 16 provides a similar focus on *projected employment change by occupation*, disaggregated by 22 Sub-Major Groups from the Standard Occupational Classification (SOC). The main features evident are:

- employment growth of 10% or more is projected for selected managerial and administrative, professional, and associate professional and technical occupations (SOC Major Groups 1, 2 and 3) in all three areas – a pattern indicative of the 'professionalisation' of employment referred to in Chapter 2; there are also sizeable projected increases in employment recorded for personal service occupations and sales occupations (it is likely that many of these will be part-time positions);

- in Inner London employment losses of at least 10% are projected for all clerical and secretarial (SOC Major Group 4), craft and skilled manual occupations (SOC Major Group 5) and for plant and machine operatives (SOC Major Group 9);

- in all three areas a decline in employment in excess of 10% is projected in other elementary occupations (unskilled occupations).

Table 15: Projected decline and growth in employment by industry (1994–2005)

Industry	Merseyside	West Midlands	Inner London
Agriculture	-	+	-
Coal	-	-	-
Oil and gas	-	-	+
Other mining	+	+	-
Food	-	-	-
Drink	-	-	-
Tobacco	+		-
Textiles	-	-	-
Clothing and leather	-		-
Wood and wood products	-	+	-
Paper, printing and publishing	-		
Manufactured fuels	-		-
Pharmaceuticals		+	-
Chemicals, etc		-	-
Rubber and plastics			
Non-metallic mineral products	-		-
Basic metals	-		-
Metal goods	-	-	-
Mechanical engineering	-	-	-
Electronics	-		-
Electrical engineering	+		-
Instruments	+		
Motor vehicles	+	+	-
Aerospace	-	-	-
Other transport equipment	-	+	-
Manufacturing nes and recycling	+	+	-
Electricity	-	-	-
Gas supply	-	-	-
Water supply	-	-	-
Construction			-
Retailing			+
Distribution nes	-		+
Hotels and catering		+	+
Rail transport	-		-
Other land transport	+	+	-
Water transport	+	+	+
Air transport	+	+	
Other transport services		+	+
Communications		-	-
Banking and finance		+	
Insurance			
Professional services	+	+	+
Computing services	+	+	+
Other business services	+	+	+
Public administration, defence	-	-	-
Education			
Health and social work	+	+	
Waste treatment	-		+
Other service activities	+		+

The shading on Tables 15 and 16 is used to highlight those industries/occupations with increase or decrease across all three areas.

Note: – decline of 10% or greater; + growth of 10% or greater; nes = not elsewhere specified.

Source: Local Economy Forecasting Model

Table 16: Projected decline and growth in employment by occupation (1994–2005)

Occupation	Merseyside	West Midlands	Inner London
1a Corporate managers and administrators	+	+	+
1b Managers/proprietors in agriculture and services	–		
2a Science and engineering professionals	+	+	+
2b Health professionals		+	+
2c Teaching professionals		–	+
2d Other professional occupations	+	+	+
3a Science and engineering associate professionals	+	+	+
3b Health associate professionals	–	–	
3c Other associate professional occupations	+	+	+
4a Clerical occupations			–
4b Secretarial occupations			–
5a Skilled construction trades	–		–
5b Skilled engineering trades			–
5c Other skilled trades			–
6a Protective service occupations	–	+	–
6b Personal service occupations	+	+	+
7a Buyers, brokers and sales representatives	+	+	+
7b Other sales occupations	+	+	+
8a Industrial plant and machinery operators	–		–
8b Drivers and mobile machinery operators	+		–
9a Other occupations in agriculture, forestry and fishing	–	+	–
9b Other elementary occupations	–	–	–

Note: – decline of 10% or greater, + growth of 10% or greater.

Source: Local Economy Forecasting Model

Table 17: Comparison of employment trends in other (unskilled) occupations and professional occupations (1981-2005)

	Merseyside		West Midlands		Inner London	
	Unskilled	*Professional*	*Unskilled*	*Professional*	*Unskilled*	*Professional*
Employment (000s)						
1981	*79.9*	42.1	*150.7*	81.3	*276.2*	159.5
1991	*49.9*	45.0	*103.5*	96.6	*191.9*	247.3
2005	*15.8*	52.4	*42.9*	106.4	*123.2*	399.1
% total employment						
1981	*13.3*	7.0	*12.1*	6.6	*12.4*	7.1
1991	*9.2*	8.3	*8.4*	7.8	*9.2*	11.9
2005	*3.1*	10.2	*3.4*	8.4	*5.5*	17.8
% change per annum						
1981-91	*-4.6*	0.7	*-3.7*	1.7	*-3.6*	4.5
1991-94	*-8.8*	-0.1	*-6.9*	-1.4	*-3.3*	2.8
1994-2005	*-7.7*	1.4	*-5.9*	1.3	*-3.1*	3.7

Source: Local Economy Forecasting Model

Table 18: Comparison of employment trends for men and women (1981-2005)

	Merseyside		West Midlands		Inner London	
	Men	Women	*Men*	Women	*Men*	Women
Total employment (000s)						
1981	*338.2*	263.7	*764.1*	486.1	*2342.2*	874.4
1991	*279.8*	265.1	*699.8*	532.7	*2120.0*	886.4
2005	*246.4*	268.0	*689.7*	582.6	*2048.1*	1058.5
Full-time employees (000s)						
1981	*287.3*	140.4	*656.0*	272.4	*1149.9*	618.8
1991	*213.4*	127.6	*552.4*	284.8	*928.4*	628.8
2005	*174.2*	119.2	*498.9*	295.1	*830.5*	705.3
Full-time employees (% of total)						
1981	*84.9*	53.2	*85.9*	56.0	*84.7*	70.8
1991	*76.3*	48.1	*78.9*	53.5	*78.0*	70.9
2005	*70.7*	44.5	*72.3*	50.7	*70.0*	66.6
Part-time employees (% of total)						
1981	*4.0*	42.0	*4.2*	39.9	*5.6*	25.7
1991	*7.1*	44.7	*6.9*	40.5	*6.5*	23.9
2005	*11.9*	47.0	*9.0*	41.0	*11.0*	26.9
Self-employed (% of total)						
1981	*11.0*	4.7	*9.9*	4.0	*9.7*	3.5
1991	*16.7*	7.1	*14.2*	6.0	*15.5*	5.2
2005	*17.5*	8.5	*18.6*	8.4	*19.0*	6.5

Source: Local Economy Forecasting Model

The extent of job losses in other (unskilled) occupations (SOC Major Group 9) since the early 1980s in the three urban areas is outlined in more detail in Table 17, and is contrasted with employment gains in professional occupations (SOC Major Group 2) over the same period. The decimation of employment in other (unskilled) occupations is readily apparent in all three urban areas. Rates of increases in employment in professional occupations have been less marked, but are indicative of the steady professionalisation of employment in these large urban areas.

There are also important gender and employment status dimensions to projected employment change. Table 18 shows the decline in employment for men – most notably for full-time employees – in each of the three large urban areas over the period from 1981-2005, contrasting with a growth in employment for women. The share of total male employment accounted for by part-time employees has increased, but remains well below the share of part-time employees among women. The proportion of those in employment who are self-employed is also projected to increase.

Occupational profiles of the unemployed

Information on the occupational breakdown of the unemployed has recently been made available on a systematic basis at the local level (see also p 45 to references to such information in the JUVOS Cohort Survey). Figures 32 and 33 show the occupational profile of the unemployed in October 1997 in two of the three large urban areas: Merseyside and Inner London. A distinction is made between the *usual* and the *sought* occupation of the unemployed, and the profiles are shown for men and women separately. The profiles for sought and usual occupations are similar; the main difference being accounted for by the greater number of unemployed persons with no usual occupation (shown as '0' in Figures 32 and 33).

Figure 32: Occupational profile of the unemployed by SOC Major Group, Merseyside (October 1997)
(a) Usual occupation

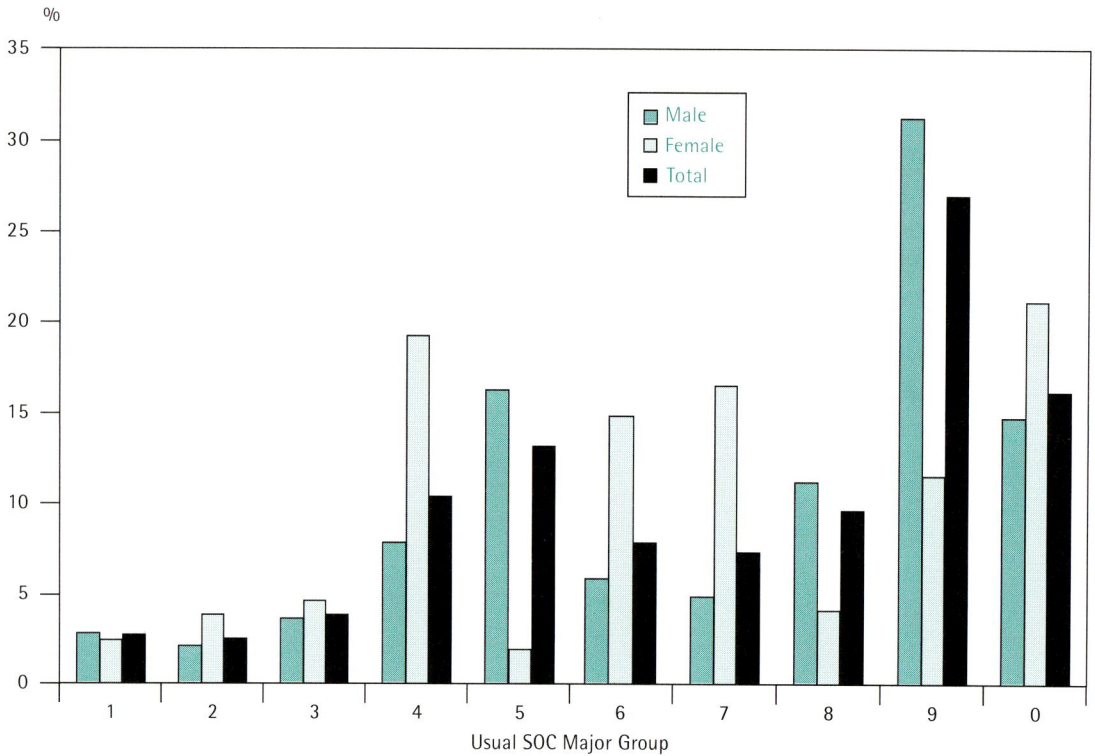

( ) ou t occupation

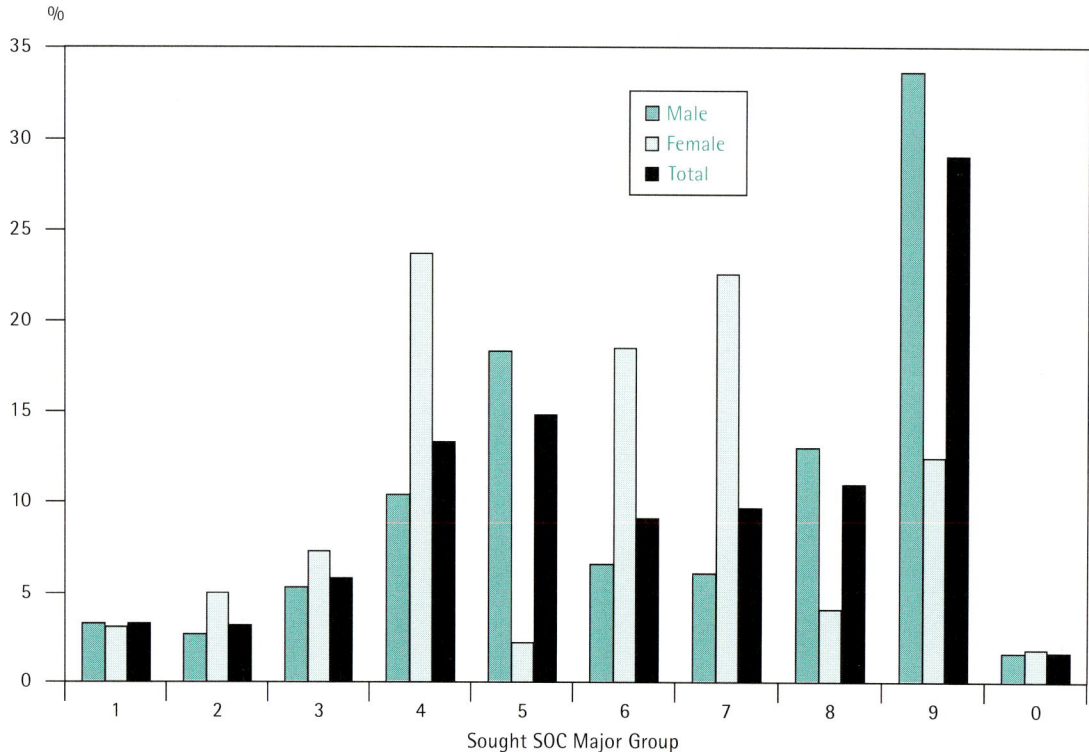

Note: See Figure 33 for key to SOC Major Groups.

Source: JUVOS claimant count unemployment count statistics disaggregated by occupation

Figure 33: Occupational profile of the unemployed by SOC Major Group, Inner London (October 1997)
(a) Usual occupation

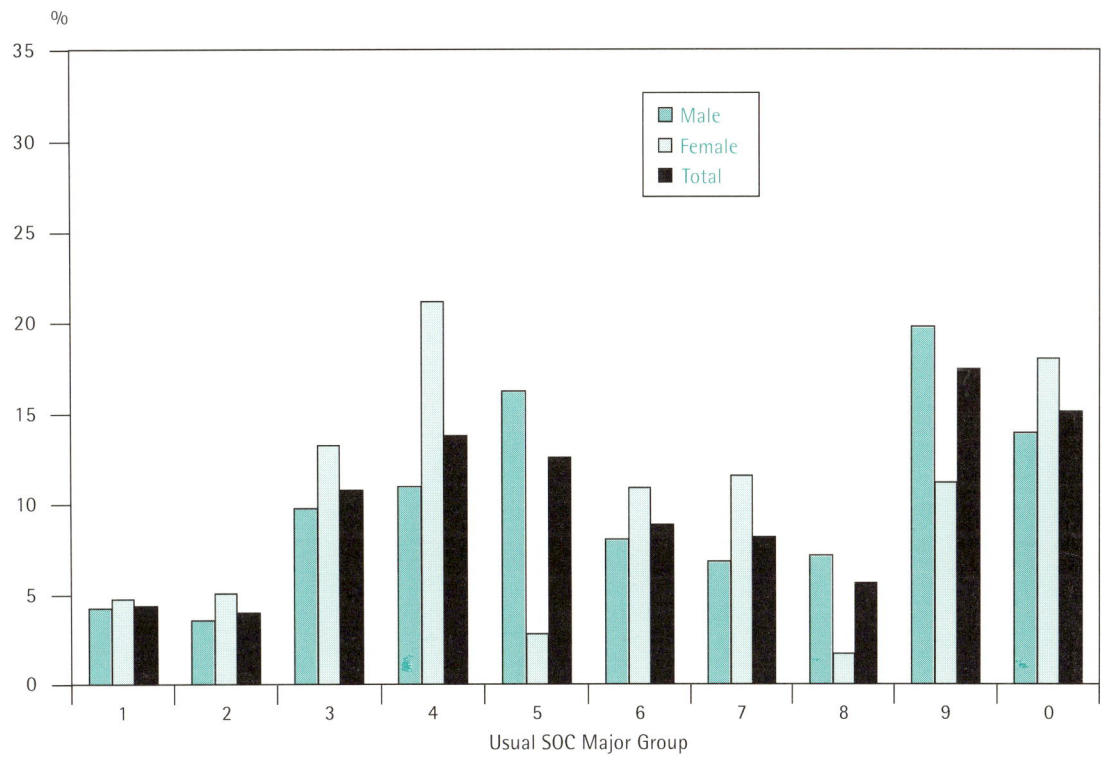

( ) ou t occupation

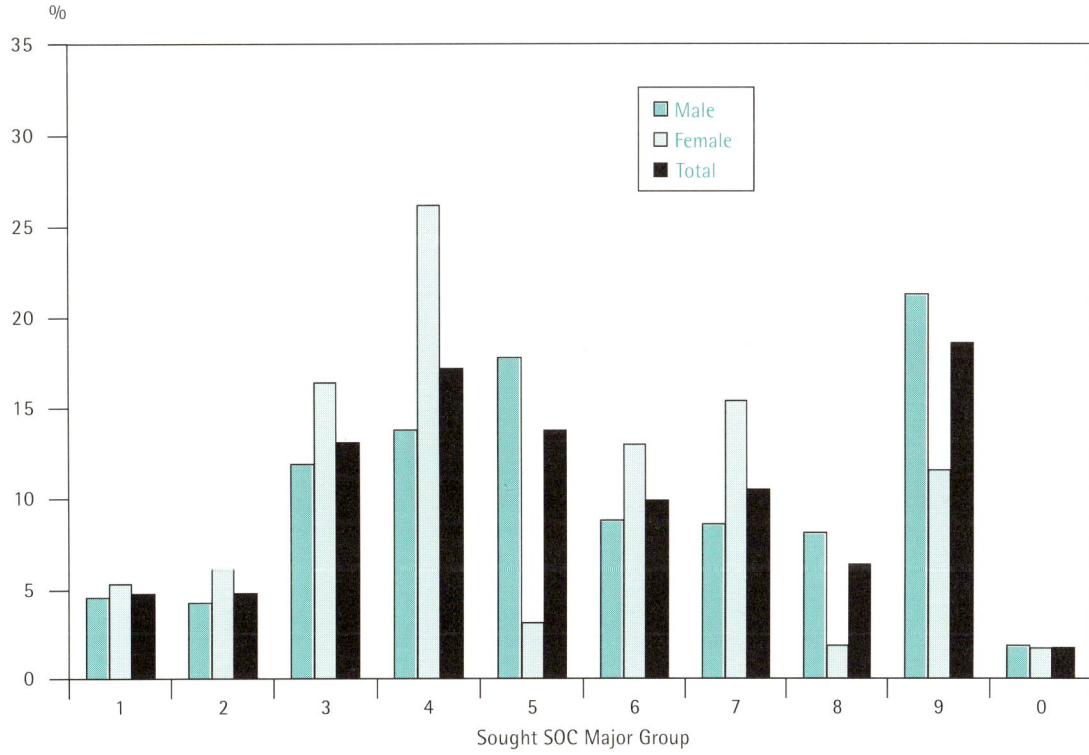

Key to SOC Major Groups: 1: Managers and administrators; 2: Professional occupations; 3: Associate professional and technical occupations; 4: Clerical and secretarial occupations; 5: Craft and skilled manual occupations; 6: Personal and protective service occupations; 7: Sales occupations; 8: Plant and machine operatives; 9: Other (unskilled) occupations.

Source: JUVOS claimant count unemployment count statistics disaggregated by occupation

The key features emerging from an examination of the occupational profile of the unemployed in these two areas are:

- The particularly large concentration of unemployed people from, or seeking work in, other (unskilled) occupations (SOC Major Group 9). Approximately one third of unemployed men in Merseyside are from this occupational group, as are one fifth in Inner London.

- There are important distinctions in the occupational profiles of unemployed men and women (which reflect occupational segregation in employment). After other (unskilled) occupations, the next largest occupational concentration of unemployed men is in craft and skilled manual occupations (SOC Major Group 5). The majority of unemployed women are seeking work in clerical and secretarial occupations (SOC Major Group 4), sales occupations (SOC Major Group 7), personal and protective service occupations (SOC Major Group 6) and other (unskilled) occupations (SOC Major Group 9).

- Very few of the unemployed are from or seeking work in higher level non-manual occupations (SOC Major Groups 1-3), which are the major employment growth areas.

Clearly, there is a *skills mismatch* in these large urban areas.

Evidence from surveys undertaken in high unemployment neighbourhoods within cities (such as the 'Pathways' areas in Merseyside [see Hasluck et al, 1997]), suggests that these skills mismatches (ie, low skills and lack of experience) are compounded by *spatial mismatches*. An emphasis on the *'local'* emerges in a number of respects: the long-term unemployed and non-employed residents of the 'Pathways' areas want *local jobs* and *local training* for *local people*. The proportions of households without cars in the high unemployment areas of Merseyside are higher than the national, regional and local averages. Therefore, the residents – and, in particular, the unemployed and non-employed – are more reliant on public transport. Coupled with concerns about the affordability of public transport, this reliance helps explain an emphasis on the 'local'. The shortage of accessible jobs (in occupational and geographical terms) is one major factor preventing people from getting jobs, and the jobs that are available are often seen to be of poor quality – notably in terms of low pay. Many residents and community groups in such areas believe that their areas suffer from negative discrimination, which produces a negative image that employers have of local people – consequently hindering their chances of obtaining employment. Moreover, *poor morale* and *apathy* are rife among many residents of the most economically and socially depressed neighbourhoods, such that between one quarter and one third of working age residents in some Pathways areas said in surveys that they would not be interested in working even if barriers to employment were removed.

Conclusions and policy implications

7

Introduction

The main task of this report has been to marshal the evidence on the changing map of joblessness in cities and regions in order to provide a context for informing and implementing policy initiatives. The analyses and findings presented in previous chapters are of relevance to:

- central government policy makers, with responsibility for formulating the general policy framework at national level;

- regional planners, who need a full understanding of regional economies in order to develop strategies to address the agenda set for the Regional Development Agencies:

  To promote sustainable economic development and social and physical regeneration and to contribute to the work of local and regional partners in areas such as training, investment, regeneration and business support. (DETR, 1997)

  and

- those in local authority economic development departments, TECs/LECs and other local agencies, with responsibility for implementing, monitoring and evaluating labour market and associated policies at the local level.

The remainder of this chapter reiterates some of the main findings of the research and the associated policy challenges, in the context of ongoing labour market trends and developments in the existing policy framework. A 'new'

broader policy approach has been called for to address the changing contours and demands of the 'new' labour market (see below). In this same spirit of *broadening* perspectives, the research emphasises the need to consider the inactive as well as the unemployed in order to derive a full picture of joblessness (p 60). The geographical distribution of joblessness is uneven (p 61), and a key challenge for policy is how to mitigate and overcome some of the problems associated with spatial concentrations of unemployment and non-employment (p 62). Finally, two key areas for future research are identified (p 64).

A 'new' labour market – a 'new' *broader* approach

The development of 'new' labour market landscapes: there have been a number of important changes in the labour market over the 1980s and 1990s (many of which can trace their origins to earlier periods). Among the most notable are:

- changes in the industrial structure – the demise of jobs in manufacturing and the growth of employment in services;

- a reduced demand for traditional skilled manual labour – predominantly men;

- a greater premium on higher level skills/ qualifications and a reduction in employment opportunities for those with no/few formal qualifications;

- increased participation in post-compulsory full-time education and increasing emphasis on life-long learning;

- a growth in flexible working and the spread of labour market insecurity;

- a greater number of women in employment;

and, the trend which is the main focus of attention here:

- *the entrenchment of high levels of unemployment and non-participation – particularly among some sub-groups and in some areas.*

The salience of skills in the 'new' labour market landscapes: the 'new' labour market landscapes which have evolved as a result of such trends have features which are rather different from those characterising the 'landscapes' of former times. The policy approaches characterising the 'old' labour market environment are likely to need reform and extension to be applicable in 'new' contexts. However, it should not be a case of a wholesale 'clear out' of the 'old' approaches to be replaced in their entirety by the 'new'; rather it is a case of changes in emphasis and of both pruning and supplementing the 'old' by introducing new initiatives. Upgrading the skills base has long been a key objective of labour market policy, and in the 'new' labour market landscapes initiatives concerned with investing in, improving standards of, and enhancing the quality of education and skills take centre stage: in the 'new' labour market landscapes skills are ever more important.

Challenging the 'skills mismatch': the analyses presented in this report have demonstrated the existence of a degree of *skills mismatch* between the characteristics of available jobs and the characteristics of the potential workers available to do those jobs. In the face of this 'skills mismatch' a variety of so-called 'supply-side' policies to enhance the skills of the unemployed and non-employed would appear appropriate. However, the evidence presented also suggests that the loss of jobs in manufacturing and in other (unskilled) occupations, is more severe in some areas than in others, and is particularly marked in (large) urban areas. The trend towards the 'professionalisation' of employment is greatest in the largest urban areas (most notably London), and it is in such areas that the degree and extensiveness of the skills mismatch is most severe. Hence, the policy challenge is greater in some areas than in others.

Employability and adaptability to cope with flexibility: alongside the primary emphasis on 'skills', the thrust of policy in the 'new' labour market landscape has been extended to encompass 'employability', 'adaptability' and 'flexibility'. The latter three attributes, along with 'skills', are the buzzwords of 'new' labour market policy. 'Employability' lies at the heart of the 'new' approach for dealing with persistent unemployment and skills mismatch (Centre for Local Economic Strategies, 1997). The challenge is to encourage the unemployed and other groups of the non-employed to improve their attractiveness to employers – largely by enhancing their formal skills and 'job readiness' – while the role of the state is to provide entitlement to a range of effective and desirable opportunities. In essence, there is increasing recognition that a 'new' approach needs to address a *wider* set of problems, with a *broader* range of policies.

Broadening perspectives on joblessness – from unemployment to non-employment

Difficulties in measuring unemployment: a distinctive feature of the analyses presented in this study is that the focus has extended beyond *unemployment* to encompass *non-employment*. Despite the continuing policy significance and widespread use of 'unemployment' as a socioeconomic indicator, it has been shown that in the face of key labour market developments, the task of conceptualising and measuring unemployment has become increasingly difficult. There is growing recognition that the 'boundaries' between the 'unemployed', the 'inactive' and the 'employed' are, in reality, not clear.

Why the unemployment figures don't work: given the ambiguity highlighted above, it is appropriate to pose the question: 'Do the unemployment figures work?' It has been established that any notion of a single 'true' measure of unemployment is likely to be flawed. The 'new' labour market is much more complex than the unemployment figures reveal. Localised job losses may lead not only to an increase in local unemployment, but also an increase in inactivity. (As noted in Chapter 3, other 'responses' are also possible.) Hence, the unemployed are not the only group of people without work. The analyses presented in previous chapters show that while there have been important cyclical variations in unemployment in the 1980s and 1990s, there has been an upward trend in inactivity rates for men in all age groups during the 1990s (for women the general trend has been one of reducing inactivity rates). Despite economic recovery from the recession of the early 1990s, the number of people who are economically inactive has risen. This is why it is important to extend the focus beyond the unemployed to incorporate (at least some of) the non-employed in order to derive a more complete picture of joblessness. Indeed, such a broader perspective on unemployment *and* non-employment is in the spirit of the trend towards a more general 'broadening' of policy remits in order to cover *all* of the economic, social and physical elements pertinent to the goals of fostering *inclusion* and *regeneration*.

The changing map of joblessness

The regional picture: adopting a geographical perspective, while some convergence in regional and urban unemployment rates was evident in the early 1990s, any trend towards convergence in non-employment is less marked than for unemployment. The reason for this is that inactivity rates are disproportionately higher in traditionally 'high unemployment' areas than in traditionally 'low unemployment' areas, in line with:

> The general rule that the greater the
> degree of labour market disadvantage,
> the less appropriate is unemployment as
> a measure of labour market slack.
> (MacKay, 1997, p 14)

As noted by Green and Hasluck (1998) on the basis of analyses at the regional level, a kind of 'double whammy' is in operation: in 'low unemployment' regions (mainly regions in southern Britain, outside London), use of the unemployment rate tends to capture a greater proportion of non-employment than in 'high unemployment' regions (mainly regions in northern Britain) where 'unemployment' captures a smaller share of total joblessness. (Moreover, complementary analyses of a wider range of Labour Force Survey data on labour market participation indicates that this broad regional geography of unemployment and non-

employment is reinforced by a similar geography of underemployment and insecure employment.) The analyses presented in this study demonstrate how a reliance solely on conventional unemployment statistics can disguise the true picture of joblessness – to different extents in different areas. Whereas unemployment rate relativities suggest a fairly optimistic picture of convergence in the geographical incidence of labour market fortunes, non-employment rates reveal a much higher incidence of joblessness in the traditional areas of high unemployment. In order for regional agencies to formulate as accurate a picture as possible of the functioning of regional economies it is important that they take account of trends in economic inactivity as well as of trends in unemployment.

The local picture: the statistics at inter- and intra-urban levels show that increasing non-employment is particularly pronounced in the larger urban areas – with some of the largest increases in the incidence of non-employment in recent years occurring in Inner London, in 'areas with inner city characteristics', and in 'concentrations of public sector housing'. A key feature emerging from the analyses conducted for this study is the deterioration of the unemployment situation in London – and particularly Inner London – relative to the national average. However, it is also apparent that a smaller share of longer duration unemployment spells in Inner London are ultimately 'translated' into inactivity than in 'mining and industrial areas' and 'urban centres' (outside London). Hence, as at the regional level, so at the local level, those agencies with responsibility for labour market policy need to focus attention not only on the stock of unemployed, but also on the economically inactive, and on flows between unemployment, inactivity and employment.

'Zooming in' – the micro area level: geographical variations in the experience of unemployment, inactivity and non-employment are most pronounced at the micro area level. The concentrations of disadvantage and deprivation in small and specific local areas have been identified as a matter of particular policy concern, (see p 62). Increases in non-employment have been greatest in those neighbourhoods characterised by a relatively high initial incidence of non-employment, and this trend is particularly pronounced for older

men – with much of this increase being accounted for by inactivity rather than unemployment. As noted by Dorling and Woodward (1996), the spatial concentration of working age adults without work – but who are also *not* unemployed – accounted for a great deal of the polarisation which occurred in British society in the 1980s.

Challenging spatial concentrations of joblessness

'Beached as the tide turns' – long-term unemployment and job losses in urban areas: it has been noted already that job losses over the last two decades have been particularly marked in large urban areas. This general pattern has been evident outside Britain – notably in the USA. There is growing recognition of the important role of changes in the structure and location of employment in understanding the plight of the urban jobless in US cities:

> The central problem facing inner city workers is not improving the flow of information about the availability of jobs, or getting to where the jobs are, or becoming job ready. The central problem is that the demand for labour has shifted from low skilled workers because of structural changes in the economy. (Wilson, 1996, p 224)

It is also in the large urban areas that problems of long-term unemployment are most severe. In Britain in some urban areas characterised by particularly severe labour market problems (such as Merseyside), not only is the likelihood of leaving unemployment lower than average, but also the likelihood of becoming unemployed is higher than average. In many other large urban areas the likelihood of leaving unemployment is lower than average, and at the intra-urban scale concentrations of chronic long-term unemployment are particularly apparent in the inner urban areas (see also Green and Owen, 1986). Across Europe there is a wish to avoid the worst excesses of the 'Americanisation' of European cities – through the spread, entrenchment and increasing isolation from the mainstream economy of 'urban backwater spaces' – characterised by the spatial concentration of the long-term jobless.

'Breaking out' – countering isolation and disaffection: in many such areas one of the key challenges for policy is how to overcome disaffection and apathy. In the areas of highest unemployment and non-employment, many of the unemployed are likely to have been through a range of different training programmes and initiatives, and have seen few positive results. If these individuals are to 'break out' of a circle of low motivation, low resources, failure and despair, they need to be convinced that any new schemes are qualitatively different. As noted by Hasluck et al (1997), it is in the early years after completion of compulsory full-time education that patterns of behaviour become established as goals and aspirations are formed, and so it is important that young people are 'locked into' the world of work if they are not to become the unemployed and inactive adults of the future. The 'New Deal' for the young unemployed, and the 'New Start' programme aimed at 14-17-year-olds who have rejected education and learning, are predicated on addressing this problem. Hence, there is increasing recognition of the need to enhance and extend the provision of outreach and specially customised services targeted on the young and disaffected which have been established in many local areas. However, it remains to be seen whether 'Welfare to Work' policies can/will offer enough 'quality opportunities' to cater for the most disadvantaged – particularly in areas of highest unemployment and job loss.

'Getting afloat' – the importance of lifelines at the local *level:* since the unemployed tend to have a lower level of resources available to them (in terms of income, availability of private transport, etc) than the employed, their outlooks tend to be more *local* in orientation: their demands tend to be for *local* jobs and *local* training. Due to localised losses of low-skilled jobs and constraints on geographical mobility, 'skills mismatches' may be further compounded by 'spatial mismatches'. Hence, opportunities and initiatives at the *local* level matter particularly for the unemployed and non-employed.

Spatial targeting and the multiagency approach: in response to the increase in the geographical concentration of poverty and exclusion, and the widespread recognition that poverty and exclusion are damaging to economic competitiveness and social cohesion, there has been an upsurge in spatially targeted, multidimensional and multiagency responses to problems of disadvantage, in Britain and other parts of Europe. Projects funded through the Single Regeneration Budget are exemplars of this trend. The announcements in 1997 of the creation of Employment Zones and Education Action Zones further underlined the importance of spatial targeting and the multiagency approach:

"Concentrated areas of unemployment still corrode some communities even though headline unemployment is falling. This is why we said in our manifesto that we would create Employment Zones, targeting help to those who need it most. In Employment Zones, new help for the long-term unemployed will be designed by local partnerships of organisations from the public, private and voluntary sectors." (Employment Minister, Andrew Smith, outlining Employment Zones, September 1997)

"Education Action Zones demonstrate our determination to raise school standards for everyone. One key feature will be a multi-agency approach working with parallel initiatives on employment, health and social services." (Education and Employment Secretary, David Blunkett, unveiling plans to set up Education Action Zones in deprived rural and inner-city areas, December 1997)

Partnerships – facilitating coordination and inclusion? or 'crossed wires' and a duplication of effort?: the establishment of multiagency partnerships at local level has gained increasing importance in recent years (in Britain and throughout the EU), and the principle of partnership is now widely accepted. The ability of local partnerships to tackle the multidimensional nature of problems in a concerted way is seen as one of the principal advantages of a partnership approach. However, while 'inclusion' is an underlying principle of partnership, in practical terms it is pertinent to pose the question whether there are (or can be) too many partners and too many overlapping initiatives to ensure effective coordination between policies, and the most

efficient use of finite resources. It is salient to note that in a wide ranging review of local partnerships Geddes (1997) concluded that there remain too few examples of partnerships which can demonstrate *lasting impact* in tackling poverty and social exclusion on a broad and multidimensional basis.

Local flexibility to meet local needs – recognising diversity: a key feature of 'New Deal' initiatives is their emphasis on 'local solutions' through 'local partnerships' for 'local needs'. Indeed, one of the concepts central to the Employment Zones initiative is 'neighbourhood match' – which is concerned with equipping participants with employability skills 'tailored' to the unique characteristics of their local labour market. However, there is a balance to be struck between short-term skills needs and the long-term interests of local and regional economies. It remains to be seen whether there will be sufficient support at the local level, over a sufficiently long period of time, to enable the development of the structures necessary for participation in economic development, and the integration of economic development with employment policy. The emphasis on 'diversity' is also important. While there are some clear similarities in the problems posed by unemployment in different areas, the key question of what the growing level of joblessness means in different local environments should not be overlooked. In some areas the non-employed will be dominated by older men who have decided to retire early – either in the face of a lack of employment opportunities for men with outdated skills, or because of 'ageism' in recruitment practices in the context of an overall employment shortfall, or (in some cases) due to the availability of attractive pension opportunities. In other areas, non-employment rates are high for men in the prime working age range, reflecting the contraction of dominant employers, for example, in coalfield areas. What is clear is that in many areas young people account for a declining share of the long-term unemployed, underlining the need for policies to focus on the prime age and older age groups as well as young people.

More than matching – challenging the jobs deficit: the scale of job losses in some local areas was outlined in Chapter 6 and reiterated on p 62 of this chapter. In the face of such large localised job losses the 'matching' of the unemployed and non-employed will be insufficient to counter problems of joblessness. A key component of a policy package to permanently lower unemployment (and non-employment) in the most disadvantaged areas must be to increase the stock of jobs (despite the main policy emphasis on a 'supply-side' approach, the role for 'demand-side' policies must not be ignored). At the local level the experience of intermediate labour markets, a range of community economic development initiatives and local 'jobs pools' (see Centre for Local Economic Strategies, 1997) may provide some useful pointers to what can be done to generate jobs. However, 'micro' strategies need to be linked to 'macro' strategies, just as 'demand-side' policies need to be implemented alongside 'supply-side' ones:

> Job creation depends on a macro-economic policy aimed at investing in planned economic growth and also substantial investment in human capital to keep up with technological change. *Only* when these are in tandem and are regulated through appropriate institutional frameworks of vocational education and training which secure a negotiated social partnership approach, can the gap between jobless growth and full-employment be bridged." (Jones, 1997, p 40)

Research needs

Finally, from a research perspective, in order to challenge the spatial concentration of joblessness as effectively as possible, two key areas for future improvement/investment of research effort may be identified:

Monitoring and analysis of labour market flows at local level: this study has highlighted the importance of 'broadening' perspectives on joblessness to encompass some sub-groups of the economically inactive as well as the unemployed if problems of exclusion are to be tackled. In order to inform policy at a local level it is important to understand and monitor the flows occurring between and within employment, unemployment and inactivity for different sub-groups of the population and in different areas. There is a need for:

- research on understanding different types and degrees of labour market attachment;

- investment in establishing information systems incorporating longitudinal statistics at individual and area levels.

Effective monitoring and evaluation: over recent years a multiplicity of local employment/ training/economic development projects have been initiated. However, effective monitoring and evaluation frameworks/systems for such labour market programmes remain underdeveloped. Yet there is a demand for indicators of outputs and outcomes in order to justify continuing support/further resources and to assess whether budgets are being expended effectively. There is a need for more investment in formulating, establishing and implementing monitoring and evaluation systems. Moreover, as various 'New Deal' initiatives come 'on stream' at local level, establishing mechanisms and systems for effective coordination between policies becomes ever more important.

References

Badcock, B. (1997) 'Restructuring and spatial polarization in cities', *Progress in Human Geography*, vol 21, pp 251-62.

Beatson, M. (1995) 'Labour market flexibility', *Employment Department Research Paper* 48, Sheffield: Employment Department.

Beatty, C. and Fothergill, S. (1996) 'Registered and hidden unemployment in areas of chronic industrial decline: The case of the UK coalfields', *Regional Studies*, vol 30, pp 627-40.

Beatty, C., Fothergill, S. and Lawless, P. (1997a) 'Geographical variation in the labour-market adjustment process: The UK coalfields 1981-91', *Environment and Planning A*, vol 29, pp 2041-60.

Beatty, C., Fothergill, S., Gore, T. and Herrington, A. (1997b) *The real level of unemployment*, Sheffield: Sheffield Hallam University.

Blotevogel, H.H. and King, R. (1996) 'European economic restructuring: demographic responses and feedbacks', *European Urban and Regional Studies,* vol 3, pp 133-59.

Bowen, D. (1990) *Shaking the iron universe*, London: Hodder & Stoughton.

Bryson, A. and McKay, S. (1994) *Is it worth working?*, London: Policy Studies Institute.

Centre for Local Economic Strategies (1997) 'Employability in the local economy', *Local Work* 1.

Champion, A.G., Green, A.E., Owen, D.W., Ellin, D.J. and Coombes, M.G. (1987) *Changing places: Britain's demographic, economic and social complexion*, London: Edward Arnold.

Commission of the European Communities (CEC) (1993) *Growth, competitiveness, employment: The challenges and the ways forward into the 21st century,* White Paper COM(93), 700 Final, CEC, Brussels.

Danziger, N. (1996) *Danziger's Britain: A journey to the edge*, London: HarperCollins.

Department of Employment (1984) 'Revised Travel-To-Work Areas', *Employment Gazette*, vol 92, no 9, Occasional Supplement 3.

Department of the Environment, Transport and the Regions (DETR) (1997) *Building partnerships for prosperity: Sustainable growth, competitiveness and employment in the English regions*, London: The Stationery Office.

Dorling, D. and Woodward, R. (1996) 'Social polarisation 1971-1991: A micro-geographical analysis of Britain', *Progress in Planning*, vol 45, pp 67-122.

Employment Policy Institute (1996) 'Introducing the Employment Audit', *Employment Audit*, vol 1, pp 1-14.

European Anti-Poverty Network (1997) 'Jobs summit: the temptation to "massage" the figures must be avoided', *Network News*, vol 52, no 1.

Fieldhouse, E.A. (1996) 'Putting unemployment in its place: using the Samples of Anonymised Records to explore the risk of unemployment in Great Britain in 1991' *Regional Studies*, vol 30, pp 119-33.

Finn, D. (1997) 'Labour's New Deal for the unemployed', *Local Economy*, vol 12, pp 247-58.

Fothergill, S. and Gudgin, G. (1982) *Unequal growth: Urban and regional employment change in the UK*, London: Heinemann.

Galster, G.C. and Killen, S.P. (1995) 'The geography of metropolitan opportunity: A reconnaissance and conceptual framework', *Housing Policy Debate*, vol 6, pp 7-43.

Geddes, M. (1997) *Partnership against poverty and exclusion? Local regeneration strategies and excluded communities in the UK*, Bristol: The Policy Press.

Goodman, A. and Webb, S. (1994) *For richer, for poorer: The changing distribution of income in the United Kingdom*, London: IFS.

Green, A.E. (1986) 'The likelihood of becoming and remaining unemployed in Great Britain, 1984', *Transactions of the Institute of British Geographers* NS 11, pp 37-56.

Green, A.E. (1995) 'A comparison of alternative measures of unemployment', *Environment and Planning A*, vol 27, pp 535-56.

Green, A.E. (1997) 'Exclusion, unemployment and non-employment', *Regional Studies*, vol 31, pp 505-20.

Green, A.E. and Hasluck, C. (1998) '(Non) participation in the labour market: Alternative indicators and estimates of labour reserve in UK regions', *Environment and Planning A*, vol 30, pp 543-58.

Green, A.E. and Owen, D.W. (1986) 'A labour market definition of disadvantage: Towards an enhanced local classification', *DfEE Research Studies* 11, London: HMSO.

Green, A.E. and Owen, D.W. (1990) 'The development of a classification of Travel-To-Work Areas', *Progress in Planning*, vol 34, pp 1-92.

Hasluck, C., Green, A.E. and Shackleton, R.E. (1997) *The Merseyside labour market: A supply-side study*, Liverpool: Labour Market Strategy Group – Government Office for Merseyside.

Haughton, G., Johnson, S., Murphy, L. and Thomas, K. (1993) *Local geographies of unemployment*, Aldershot: Avebury.

Holzer, H.J. (1991) 'The spatial mismatch hypothesis: What has the evidence shown?', *Urban Studies*, vol 28, pp 105-22.

House of Commons Employment Committee (1996) *Unemployment and employment statistics*, London: HMSO.

Hutton, W. (1995) 'The 30-30-40 society', *Regional Studies*, vol 29, pp 719-21.

Institute for Employment Research (IER) (1996) *Review of the economy and employment: Labour Market Assessment*, Coventry: IER, University of Warwick.

Jones, M. (1997) 'Implementing Labour's New Deal: Lessons from the policy past', in Regional Studies Association, *Community economic development: Linking the grassroots to regional economic development*, London: Regional Studies Association, pp 37-41.

Kain, J.F. (1968) 'Housing segregation, negro employment, and metropolitan decentralization', *The Quarterly Journal of Economics*, vol 82, pp 175-97.

Kain, J.F. (1992) 'The spatial mismatch hypothesis: Three decades later', *Housing Policy Debate*, vol 3, pp 371-460.

Kasarda, J.D. and Kwok-fai, Ting (1996) 'Joblessness and poverty in America's central cities: Causes and policy prescriptions', *Housing Policy Debate*, vol 7, pp 387-419.

Kunzmann, K.R. (1996) 'Euro-megalopolis or themepark Europe?', *International Planning Studies*, vol 1, pp 143-63.

Laux, R. (1997) 'Measuring labour market attachment using the Labour Force Survey', *Labour Market Trends*, vol 105, pp 407-14.

Lee, P. (1994) 'Housing and spatial deprivation: relocating the underclass and the new urban poor', *Urban Studies*, vol 31, pp 1191-209.

Lewis, J. and Townsend, A.R. (1989) *The North-South divide: Regional economic change in Britain in the 1980s*, London: Paul Chapman.

McRae, S. (1997) 'Household and labour market change: Implications for the growth of inequality in Britain', *British Journal of Sociology*, vol 48, pp 384-405.

MacKay, R.R. (1997) 'Work and nonwork: A more difficult labour market', Paper presented at the European Urban and Regional Research Network Conference, Frankfurt Oder, Germany, September.

Martin, R. (1993) 'Remapping British regional policy: The end of the North-South divide', *Regional Studies*, vol 27, pp 797-805.

May, N. (1997) *Challenging assumptions: Gender issues in urban regeneration*, York: Joseph Rowntree Foundation/York Publishing Services.

Mead, L.M. (1989) 'The logic of workfare: The underclass and work policy', *The Annals of the American Academy of Political and Social Science*, vol 501, pp 156-69.

Meadows, P. (1996) *Work out – or work in?: Contributions to the future of work debate*, York: Joseph Rowntree Foundation.

Murray, C. (1984) *Losing ground: American social policy 1950-1980*, New York: Basic Books.

Nicaise, I., Bollens, J., Dawes, L., Laghaei, S., Thaulow, I., Verdie, M. and Wagner, A. (1995) *Pitfalls and dilemmas in labour market programmes for disadvantaged groups and how to avoid them*, Aldershot: Avebury.

Nickell, S. and Bell, B. (1995) 'The collapse in demand for the unskilled and unemployment across the OECD', *Oxford Review of Economic Policy*, vol 11, pp 40-62.

Owen, D.W., Gillespie, A.E. and Coombes, M.G. (1984) 'Job shortfalls in British local labour market areas: A classification of labour supply and demand trends', *Regional Studies*, vol 18, pp 469-88.

Ramprakash, D. (1994) 'Poverty in the countries of the European Union', *Journal of European Social Policy*, vol 4, pp 117-28.

Regional Policy Commission (1996) *Renewing the regions: Strategies for regional economic development*, Sheffield: Sheffield Hallam University.

Royal Statistical Society (1995) 'The measurement of unemployment in the UK', *Journal of the Royal Statistical Society*, vol 158, pp 363-417.

Sly, F. (1994) 'Economic activity results from the 1991 Labour Force Survey and Census of Population', *Employment Gazette*, vol 102, pp 87-96.

Smith, D. (1989) *North and South*, London: Penguin.

Steel, D. (1997) 'Producing monthly estimates of unemployment and employment according to the International Labour Office definition', *Journal of the Royal Statistical Society*, vol 160, pp 5-46.

Townsend, A.R. (1993) 'The urban-rural cycle in the Thatcher growth years', *Transactions of the Institute of British Geographers* NS 18, pp 207-21.

Townsend, A.R. (1997) *Making a living in Europe*, London: Routledge.

Turok, I. (1997) 'Travel-To-Work Areas and the measurement of unemployment', *Occasional Paper* 38, Glasgow: Centre for Housing Research and Urban Studies, University of Glasgow.

US Department of Housing and Urban Development (1997) *The state of the cities*, Washington DC: US Department of Housing and Urban Development.

Wallace, M. and Denham, C. (1996) 'The ONS classification of local and health authorities of Great Britain', *ONS Studies on Medical and Population Subjects*, vol 59, London: HMSO.

Webster, D. (1997) 'The "L-U Curve": On the non-existence of a long-term unemployment trap and its implications for policies on employment and area regeneration', *Occasional Paper* 36, Glasgow: Centre for Housing Research and Urban Studies, University of Glasgow.

Wilson, W.J. (1987) *The truly disadvantaged: The inner city, the underclass and public policy*, Chicago: University of Chicago Press.

Wilson, W.J. (1996) *When work disappears: The world of the new urban poor*, New York: Knopf.

Woolford, C. and Denman, J. (1993) 'Measures of unemployment: The claimant count and the LFS compared', *Employment Gazette*, vol 101, pp 455-64.

Blair, T. (1997) Speech by the Prime Minister, Tony Blair, at the Aylesbury Estate, Southwark, 2 June.

Appendix A:
Geographical frameworks

Geographical units at the local level

In this study use is made of:

- *280 local labour market areas (LLMAs)*: these are a set of urban-centred regions which are relatively self-contained in terms of journey-to-work flows from the CURDS Functional Regions framework (Champion et al, 1987). Use is made of classifications which distinguish LLMAs according to regional location ('North' or 'South' of a line from the Severn to Lincolnshire), urban size and hierarchical status.

- *322 travel-to-work areas (TTWAs)*: these are a set of local labour market areas derived in 1984 on behalf of the Department of Employment for the presentation of unemployment and employment data (Department of Employment, 1984). Each TTWA represents a grouping of wards which forms a relatively self-contained commuting area. In this study use is made of an a priori classification of TTWAs which distinguishes between groups of TTWAs on the basis of regional location, urban size and hierarchical status (see Green and Owen, 1990).

- *459 local authority districts (LADs)*: these are administrative areas derived from the 1974 reorganisation of local government. The LADs vary quite markedly in size – in terms of population and geographical area, and in terms of self-containment in terms of commuting flows. In this study use is made of an ONS cluster analysis classification of LADs, which distinguishes between LADs on the basis of a range of socioeconomic and demographic variables (Wallace and Denman, 1996). The six 'families', 12 'groups' and 34 'clusters' in this classification are shown in the next table.

ONS classification of local authority districts of Great Britain

Family	Group	Cluster	Most typical LAD
Rural areas	Scotland	Highlands and Islands	Moray
		Uplands and agriculture	Berwickshire
	Coast and country	Remoter England and Wales	South Shropshire
		Heritage coast	Carrick
		Accessible amenity	Purbeck
	Mixed urban and rural	Towns in country	Mendip
		Industrial margins	Alyn and Deeside
Prospering areas	Most prosperous	Concentrations of prosperity	Surrey Heath
		Established high status	Tandridge
	Growth areas	Satellite towns	Rugby
		Growth corridors	Aylesbury Vale
		Areas with transient populations	Cherwell
		Metropolitan overspill	Broxbourne
		Market towns	Wansdyke
Maturer areas	Services and education	University towns	Brighton
		Suburbs	Croydon
	Resort and retirement	Traditional seaside towns	Shepway
		Smaller seaside towns	East Devon
Urban centres	Mixed economies	Established service centres	Hereford
		Scottish towns	East Lothian
		New and expanding towns	Northampton
	Manufacturing	Pennine towns	Bolton
		Areas with large ethnic minorities	Bradford
Mining and industrial areas	Ports and industry	Areas with inner city characteristics	Kingston Upon Hull
		Coastal industry	Kirkcaldy
		Glasgow and Dundee	Clydebank
		Concentrations of public sector housing	Motherwell
	Coalfields	Mining and industry, England	Rotherham
		Mining and services, Wales	Swansea
		Former mining areas, Wales and Durham	Wear Valley
Inner London	Inner London	Central London	Camden
		Cosmopolitan outer boroughs	Waltham Forest
		Inner city boroughs	Southwark
		Newham and Tower Hamlets	(both dissimilar from any other LAD)

Appendix B: Producing local area estimates

This Appendix provides details of some of the technical procedures and considerations involved in generating estimates of socioeconomic change at the local scale.

Producing estimates of economic activity change between 1981 and 1991

The Census of Population is the most comprehensive source of socioeconomic information on the population of Great Britain, having complete geographical and population coverage, in contrast to survey data sets, such as the Labour Force Survey. Its main drawback is that it is only taken once every 10 years. Nevertheless, it is useful in providing an overview of changes over a decade in various phenomena at a range of spatial scales.

However, the calculation of change between two Censuses is not straightforward, due to changes between Censuses in the definitions used, the boundaries of area units for which data are collected, and the precise definition of the resident population. (In 1971, this was the enumerated population, in 1981 usual residents, and in 1991 usual residents plus visitors.) Moreover, the extent of underenumeration in the Census was more than twice as great in 1991 than 1981. For this study, a set of estimates of the population disaggregated by age and sex and by economic status was generated by adjusting Small Area Statistics data from the 1981 and 1991 Censuses of Population.

Data were extracted for the smallest areas to be analysed (electoral wards) and aggregated up to different spatial scales, making use of

information derived from the Area Master File for the 1981 Census and definitions of local labour market areas. Electoral wards changed their boundaries between 1981 and 1991, but it was decided to use 1981 electoral wards as the basis for the study, because of the availability of 1991 Census data reaggregated to 1981 ward boundaries on the Manchester computer system (provided by CURDS as an output from an ESRC-funded research project). This choice slightly limited the amount of detail available in the age breakdown of economic activity, since the 1991 data had been created by aggregating Small Area Statistics data for enumeration districts, which had a less detailed age breakdown of economic activity than the 1991 Local Base Statistics or the 1981 Small Area Statistics. (In the 1991 data set five-year age groups were aggregated in the 34-44, 45-54 and 65+ age ranges, in contrast to the 1981 data, in which five-year age groups were used throughout the age range.)

Given the differences in population definition and coverage between the two Censuses, it is possible to generate quite misleading measures of population change by simply comparing unadjusted data from the two Censuses. Fortunately, an alternative source of information on the changing population of local areas is available, in the form of the Office for National Statistics and General Register Office (Scotland) mid-year (30 June) estimates of the population by age and sex for the 459 local authority districts existing in Great Britain from 1974 to the mid-1990s (before the introduction of Unitary Authorities). These are created using Census data and information on births, deaths and migration, and adjust for the Census underenumeration of the population.

Here, the Census population data for electoral wards was adjusted, by constraining the total population summed across all wards in the district to be the same as the mid-year population estimate, for each age group and sex. This procedure was applied to both the 1981 and 1991 data. Having adjusted the population data, the numbers economically active and unemployed in each age group were adjusted by calculating the proportion of the age group economically active or unemployed using the unadjusted Census data, and then applying these proportions to the adjusted population data.

Producing estimates of employment change from the Special Workplace Statistics, 1981 and 1991

Data were extracted from Set B of the Special Workplace Statistics for 1981 and 1991, using the data files available on the MIDAS computer system at Manchester. The 1991 data were converted to a 1981 ward area base, using a 1991 ward to 1981 ward converter derived from an allocation of 1991 Census enumeration districts to 1981 Census wards (produced by Daniel Dorling and made available via MIDAS).

Unfortunately, 1981 Special Workplace Statistics data are not available for Scotland (either at Manchester or on NOMIS), and hence analysis of this data must be limited to England and Wales.

One major difficulty in using the data is in generating reliable estimates of change in employment between 1981 and 1991. This is because the data are on a *workplace* basis – that is, the data enumerate the number of persons (actually a 10% sample) contacted by the Census and with a workplace in each area. There is no independent source of reliable information on the number of people working in each ward (or aggregate thereof) comparable with the mid-year estimates data used for scaling up the resident population data. Thus, employment change measures will be distorted by problems such as the greater degree of Census underenumeration in 1991 than 1981, problems with geographical coding of workplace (and differences in the degree of accuracy of this procedure between 1981 and 1991), and the influence of sampling error.

The variables extracted from the Special Workplace Statistics were selected to be as comparable as possible between 1981 and 1991; thus employment classified by social class, socioeconomic group and 1980 Standard Industrial Classification (SIC) industry division were selected, broken down by gender (and self-employment/employed status for industry divisions).